COUNTRY BUSES

VOLUME TWO 1950–1959

COUNTRY BUSES

VOLUME TWO 1950–1959

Laurie Akehurst

Capital Transport

Author's Note

When this work was first envisaged it was planned to span two volumes but as it developed the decision was made to go to three volumes in order to include a greater number of photographs, many reproduced in a larger size. Volume One dealt with the early days, the formation of the London Passenger Transport Board and the vicissitudes of war and its immediate aftermath. This volume considers the 1950s which was a decade when the fortunes of London Transport Country Buses changed considerably. The decade opened with a great demand for bus travel and optimistic plans for the renewal of the vehicle fleet. Passenger levels peaked in the mid-1950s after which time a steady decline in demand became established which was exacerbated by the disastrous six week strike in 1958. By the end of the decade, in a period of post-war prosperity, car ownership levels had made considerable inroads into the demand for bus travel, and London Transport's aims of providing an adequate service and covering its costs were becoming conflicting requirements.

In this period route developments became extremely complex, especially when dealing with the new towns. I have endeavoured to provide a comprehensive overview of all route alterations but, no doubt, some minor variations may have escaped the net and if the reader's favourite special journey to work or school has been omitted I can only apologise.

The production of this volume would not have been possible without valuable assistance from others. I am especially indebted to Philip Hopcroft who kindly read through the text, checked cross references and raised a number of points which I was able to clarify. Over the many years of research for this work my very good friend, the late Mervyn Gibson, was always willing to discuss the many points that I raised. I am also indebted to Caroline Warhurst, the LT Museum librarian, in respect of assistance gratefully received. Special thanks must also go to Alan Cross and Mick Webber for their assistance with photographs. Thanks also go to Hugh Taylor who made a number of photographs taken by Ron Wellings available for publication.

For any readers requiring additional information on vehicle types I would readily recommend *RT* by Ken Blacker and *RF* by the late Ken Glazier and the *London Bus File* series, all published by Capital Transport though all now out of print. The story of Green Line coach operation has been told in my book *London Transport Green Line* and the events after 1970 have been covered in *London Country* by David Stewart and myself, both of which were published by Capital Transport.

Watford, April 2014   Laurie Akehurst

First published 2014

ISBN 978-1-85414-377-8

Published by Capital Transport Publishing
www.capitaltransport.com

Printed by Parksons Graphics

Overleaf: The allocation of new RLHs to Addlestone enabled some wartime STL19s to be sent to Godstone and Reigate where they displaced the 'Godstone' STLs. The STL19 type consisted of twenty low-height bodies which were placed on existing randomly numbered chassis in 1942. STL 2311 is seen in all over green livery working on route 410. *F.G. Reynolds*

Contents

Bus stop at Watford Junction in the early 1950s. *Alan B. Cross*

CHAPTER 1 DEVELOPMENTS 1950–1953

RT 1092 was one of a batch of 21 Weymann bodied RTs to be allocated to Hatfield Garage in January 1949. When new it would have had the cream upper deck window surrounds and reduced area blinds. The all over Lincoln green livery and the fitting of full blinds enhanced its appearance considerably. The bus is seen returning to its home garage as a duplicate on route 303A. *Geoff Rixon*

The early 1950s was a period when things looked optimistic for London Transport in general and the Country Buses and Coaches operating department in particular. Plans had been devised to replace both the pre-war fleet and the austerity vehicles which would lead to Country Buses operating a standardised fleet with just four vehicle types. New bus overhauling facilities would be established at Aldenham and a new design of garage would become a standard for the future. The population of the Country Area was set to expand considerably under the terms of the Town and Country Planning Act, 1947. To stop urban sprawl a green belt was defined around London and outside this area a number

of new towns were to be established. Those in the Executive's area were at Crawley, Harlow, Hatfield, Hemel Hempstead, Stevenage and Welwyn Garden City. In addition London County Council overspill housing estates were to be built at Aveley, Borehamwood, Merstham, Sheerwater and South Oxhey. In the Grays area the Executive's boundary would be redrawn to include Tilbury which was to involve the taking over of a number of Eastern National routes. On the negative side staff shortage, the increase in television ownership and the abolition of wartime petrol rationing for private motorists in May 1950 would have adverse effects on passenger growth.

Some minor changes to services applied from 4th January 1950 when works journeys on routes 303/A, 330 and 340 were provided to De Havilland's Propeller Factory in Manor Road, Hatfield. On 11th January route 344 (Watford Met. Station – Brockley Hill Works) was re-routed between Watford Met. Station and Pond Cross Roads away from Rickmansworth Road to run via Hagden Lane, Whippendell Road, Market Street and High Street. Certain journeys were run via Clarendon Road and Watford Junction instead of Pond Cross Roads as route 344A. One week later all Englefield Green short workings on route 441 were projected from Kingsley Avenue to Larchwood Drive. On 1st March 1950 one journey on route 462B (Walton – Vickers Works) was extended to Cobham on school days. On the same date journeys from Dartford to Crayford Ness which had run as 480 were transferred to route 486.

London Transport's programme of introducing routes covering previously unserved roads, which had commenced in 1948, continued with route 449 which was introduced on 1st March 1950 from Dorking (Bus Station) to Ewhurst via Chart Downs, Holmwood thence over the 414 to Capel and continuing via Ockley. On 30th August 1950 route 381 was introduced between Epping and Toothill. The introduction of this route had been delayed until Essex County Council had made improvements to the roads traversed. The original intention was that the route would continue to Ongar but the state of the roads beyond Toothill was considered unsuitable and it was not until 1957 that a very short-lived extension was made.

From 12th April 1950 certain works journeys on routes 417 and 484 terminating at Colnbrook were projected to Colnbrook By-Pass (Procea Works). The summer programme applied from 10th May 1950 when the following seasonal enhancements were introduced:

368 St Albans Garage – Whipsnade Zoo. Re-introduced for summer season.

376 Luton – Kensworth. Extended on Sundays to Whipsnade Zoo.

442 Slough Station – Farnham Royal via Stoke Poges. Extended on Monday to Saturday to Burnham Beeches.

474 Slough Station – Burnham Beeches via Bath Road Sunday only. Re-introduced for summer season.

Where necessary the service levels were increased on other routes serving places of interest which attracted additional passengers in the summer.

In addition the following service changes took place:

327 Hertford – Nazeing Gate. Extended to Nazeingwood Common.

355 St Albans – Borehamwood. Intermediately re-routed in St Albans away from St Stephens Hill and Watling Street to serve Cottonmill Estate.

464 Holland – Westerham. Certain short journeys between Holland and Oxted (Police Station) extended to Barrow Green Road.

466 Staines (SR Station) – Virginia Water Station via Stroude. Certain journeys re-routed at Virginia Water Cross Roads to terminate at Knowle Hill, replacing route 469.

466A New route Englefield Green (Larchwood Drive) – Knowle Hill. (T)

469 Staines (Bridge Street) – Virginia Water (Wheatsheaf) or Knowle Hill via Thorpe. Journeys to Knowle Hill withdrawn.

477 Orpington (Kelvin Parade) or Chelsfield (Saturday and Sunday) – Dartford and Monday to Friday shuttle service provided between Orpington Station and Goddington Lane. Extended in Dartford from Market Street to Temple Hill Estate via East Hill replacing route 481.

481 Dartford Garage and Temple Hill Estate route withdrawn.

Route 372 between Hertford and Welwyn Garden City had been introduced on 19th May 1948 and passenger traffic developed to such an extent that the Cubs were replaced by T types from 10th May 1950. C 52 is seen in Welwyn Garden City some time before the change. *M. Morant*

Route 327 gained a short extension on 10th May 1950 from Nazeing Gate to Nazeingwood Common. STL 1680 is seen in Hoddesdon heading for the new destination. One of the first batch of roof box STLs, the bus was new to Tottenham Garage in November 1936 and had been painted green in September 1944. *M.G. Webber collection*

Certain short journeys on route 464 between Holland and Oxted Police Station were extended to Barrow Green Road on 10th May 1950. C 14 together with its proud driver is recorded working one such journey. *Alan B. Cross*

At an early stage during the Second World War bus building activities had been frozen so when in 1941 London Transport was allocated some 34 AEC chassis they were generally referred to as "unfrozens". There was a delay in body building at the time so the decision was taken to use works float bodies thus the batch STL 2648 – 2681 appeared with a variety of bodies. STL 2679 was fitted with one of the early bodies coded STLI/I. The bus is seen working on Watford local route 332 which was extended to serve Oxhey Estate on 7th June 1950.

On 7th June route 332 (Cassiobury Park Estate – Bushey Station) was extended to the newly developing Oxhey Estate via Eastbury Road, Wood Waye and Green Lane to Prestwick Road (Little Oxhey Lane) using STLs instead of the 4Q4s.

Staff shortage was a continuing problem with London Transport. One week in 1950 the Country Buses and Coaches department was short of 61 drivers and 126 conductors. The approved establishment for the department at the time was 2,952 drivers and 2,866 conductors. The problem was usually acute in towns where plenty of opportunities in industry existed and the two Watford (High Street and Leavesden Road) garages were short of 16 drivers and 42 conductors. Services were maintained through the goodwill of staff in working overtime and rest-days. In an attempt to create the extra resources required for the 332 extension some work on the 351 was transferred from Watford High Street to St Albans. This action was not well received by the staff at St Albans who promptly banned overtime and rest-day working. As a result the 351 work was put back to Watford High Street on 9th August. There was a further ban on overtime and rest-day working at Luton and the Watford garages from 5th September until 20th December which inevitably caused the cancellation of many journeys. This action caused service levels to be reduced on routes 306, 311, 335 and 361 from 8th November until 17th January 1951 (27th December 1950 in the case of route 361) by which time the staff position had improved. In addition three hired coaches at Watford High Street and four at Luton were employed, in some cases to work supplementary unadvertised journeys. Those at Watford were discontinued from 29th January and at Luton from 19th February 1951.

Some further service revisions took place on 5th July 1950 which involved the following route changes:

386 Hitchin – Bishop's Stortford. Intermediately re-routed between Standon and Little Hadham away from the A120 to serve Wellpond Green.

395A Hertford – Ware (Musley Hill). Extended to Fanham Common forming a loop working.

399 Hertford – Coopersale Street. One morning journey extended to Coopersale Common.

459 New route introduced between Uxbridge and Richings Park Estate worked by Ts off route 458.

The extension of the 399 to Coopersale Common had been requested by the local people but what they thought of just one journey being provided has not been recorded. The service to Richings Park Estate had previously been provided by Central Area route 220 which had been withdrawn during the early months of the war.

New route 459 from Uxbridge to Richings Park Estate at Iver was introduced on 5th July 1950 using T types off route 458. Green Line coach T 658 is seen at Uxbridge Station in 1951 together with RT 3198 on route 455 working a short journey to Gerrards Cross.
Alan B. Cross

Guildford local route 448A was introduced 9th August 1950 using buses off route 448. Now preserved CR 14 is seen in green livery at Onslow Street Bus Station in May 1953. *Alan B. Cross/ Allen T. Smith*

On 9th August 1950 works service 376A (Dunstable Sphinx Works – Kensworth) gained an extension to Studham. A new route, 448A, was introduced in Guildford between Onslow Street Bus Station and Pewley Way. No additional buses were required as the Cubs on route 448 were used. This introduction had been deferred from 7th June. The winter programme applied from 27th September when new timetables were introduced on most services with the usual seasonal withdrawals. The decision to place the 'Godstone' STLs back into service, following their displacement by RLHs, enabled a number of route revisions in the Addlestone area to take place. The full route alterations were:

391A St Albans (Townsend) – Hill End Hospital or Hill End Station. Extended in Townsend from Waverley Road to Connaught Road.

436 Staines – Woking. Extended to Guildford via Burpham replacing route 438. (RLH and low-height STL)

436A Ripley – Woking. Extended to Staines. (RLH and low-height STL)

436B Woking – Guildford via Merrow, route withdrawn.

438 Woking – Guildford via Burpham, route withdrawn.

463 Walton – Woking via Weybridge and Woodham. Extended to Guildford via Merrow covering route 436B. (low-height STL)

496 Kings Farm Estate – Gravesend – Vale Road – Northfleet. Monday to Friday pm peak hour extension to Dartford withdrawn.

It had become custom and practice over the years to supplement the scheduled buses with a number of unscheduled duplicates. For the 1950 winter programme an additional 27 buses were provided on Monday to Friday, 58 on Saturday and nine on Sunday.

London Transport's operating costs continued to rise and under the terms of the Passenger Transport Act, 1947 applications for fares revisions had to be submitted to the Transport Tribunal for approval. The latter body granted an application for a rise on all London Transport road and rail services from 1st October 1950. This was a rather more severe increase than in February 1947 and while the minimum fare remained at 1½d. other fares rose between ½d. and 7d. The highest fare of 2s 7d. was increased to 3s 2d. As far as Country Buses was concerned all return tickets, except those in areas where other operators' fare scales applied and all workmen's return facilities were abolished. These return and workmen's return fares were by no means universal across the system but applied in situations where they had been inherited by London Transport from acquired operators. The loss of workmen's facilities was offset by the introduction across the system of an early morning single fare which was available for journeys completed before 8am. For example where the ordinary single fare was between 3d and 1s 1d. the EMS fare was 2d. Vehicle time cards were clearly marked up to which point these booking

The introduction of the new RLH low-height double-deckers earlier in 1950 had allowed the 'Godstone' STLs dating from 1934 to be placed into store. They were found to be in such good condition that they were placed back in service on 27th September 1950 in consequence of a major revision of routes working from Addlestone and Guildford garages. STL 1046 is seen at Staines West Station prior to working to Walton on route 461. *Alan B. Cross*

When RTs were equipped with full blinds the main display for route 321 initially appeared with Luton incorrectly shown as an intermediate point as seen on Cravens bodied RT 1407. The display was subsequently amended, for what it was worth, to show Lantern Fields instead as displayed on RT 4033. Both views were taken in Luton. *Alan B. Cross*

New route 370A was introduced on 14th February 1951 to serve the rapidly expanding LCC estate at Aveley. The blinds of RT 3183 seen standing in Grays are a complete shambles. The "B" box has not been masked to suit the reduced area blind thus two destinations are displayed. The totally unnecessary separate route number blind shows 371A and the canopy blind is set to 371. Poor presentations such as this were by no means untypical of Grays Garage. *Alan B. Cross*

were available. EMS fares were not available on routes or sections of routes subject to other operators' fare scales. The only daily return tickets were available on sections of routes 339, 441 and 455 and on routes 359 and 364 throughout. Following negotiations with Birch Brothers, monthly return fares were introduced on sections of routes 303 and 303A from 12th November.

In the pre-war period Christmas Day services had only been provided on a handful of routes in Gravesend and Slough due to arrangements inherited by London Transport. The war saw a vast increase in the provision of such services which were continued into the post-war period. On Christmas Day 1950 a service was provided on 87 routes across the network between approximately 8.30am and 5.00pm while on Boxing Day a full Sunday service was operated. Christmas Day operation was expensive to provide as staff were entitled to enhanced rates of pay and passenger usage was carefully monitored with a view to withdrawing any under-used journeys in subsequent years.

With a start made on housing in Harlow New Town, additional passengers were using route 396 and as a result of requests made by local authorities a number of journeys on the route were revised to double run to serve Epping Station on Monday to Saturday from 10th January 1951. Housing development at Aveley, where about 60 to 70 new houses were being occupied each week, accounted for the introduction of route 370A on 14th February. The route ran somewhat indirectly from Grays to Ockendon Station via West Thurrock, Stonehouse Corner and Aveley. Daily works journeys were also provided under the same route number from Purfleet Station to Ockendon Station which joined the main route at Stonehouse Corner.

The last route to be introduced at this period covering previously unserved roads was the 315 which commenced on Good Friday, 23rd March 1951. The route ran from Welwyn Garden City Station to Wheathampstead (Marford Estate) via Ayot St Lawrence where some journeys terminated. The route's main function was to serve the home of the late George Bernard Shaw, the Irish playwright, which had recently opened to the public. The Executive had previously refused consent for Silverline Coaches to provide a service from Welwyn Garden City to Ayot St Lawrence. No Monday or Tuesday service was provided on the route and passenger levels failed to come up to expectations which resulted in its early withdrawal. It ran for the last time on 12th August 1951 and had been worked by one Cub from Hatfield Garage.

Short-lived route 315 was introduced on 23rd March 1951 primarily to serve the home of the late George Bernard Shaw at Ayot St Lawrence which had recently opened to the public. C 23 is seen at Welwyn Garden City with an RT behind working to New Barnet on route 340. *R.K. Blencome*

On 4th April 1951 route 351 (St Albans – Uxbridge) was extended from St Albans to Harpenden. Route 386 was intermediately re-routed between Hitchin and Stevenage away from the main road through Little Wymondley to serve Titmore Green and Todd's Green and to enter Stevenage via Fishers Green Road. The Thursday service which ran between Buntingford and Bishop's Stortford was increased and certain positioning journeys that had run on Thursday, Saturday and Sunday between Hertford and Standon Station or Buntingford as 331 were now run as route 386A via Ware, Wareside and Widford, as route 350 to Hadham Ford and then over route 386 via Wellpond Green to Standon. The few journeys that continued to Buntingford did so via Westmill rather than via Braughing as the 386.

Some minor alterations took place on 25th April when a journey on route 330 was projected to St Albans Marshalswick Estate for the purpose of interworking on to route 343 and a journey on route 398 was extended from Beaconsfield to Holtspur for the purpose of inter-working with route 373. On 9th May journeys were provided on route 371A between Grays and Hedley's Works at West Thurrock. These work-ings left the main line of route to run via Stone Ness Road to the works.

Passenger numbers on seasonal route 368 between St Albans and Whipsnade Zoo had not come up to management's expectations in 1950 so an alternative way of providing the service was found. Route 313 (Enfield – St Albans) was seasonally extended to Whipsnade. In order to

serve St Peters Street and to facilitate crew changes, the Whipsnade journeys double ran via Chequer Street, St Peters Street and the garage forecourt returning to Mayles Corner. The seasonal extension was introduced on Whit-Sunday, 13th May with new RTs replacing the STLs. Route 368 had run over the Easter weekend so its last day of operation had been Easter Monday, 26th March 1951.

Leyland Cubs C 94 with a Weymann body and C 15 with a Short Brothers body are seen at St Marys Square, Hitchin working on routes 383 and 386 respectively. C 94 is now preserved as part of the London Transport Museum collection. *Alan B. Cross*

When route 313 was extended seasonally from St Albans to Whipsnade Zoo on 13th May 1951 it lost STLs in favour of RTs. RT 1104 is seen in St Peters Street, St Albans in February 1953. *Alan B. Cross*

The summer service revision programme for 1951 came a little later than usual on 13th June and included the following route alterations:

308 Hertford – Newgate Street. Extended to Cuffley Station.

320 Watford – Boxmoor Station via Leverstock Green. Intermediately re-routed at Adeyfield to serve new development at Longlands.

344B New route, one journey in this direction only: Watford (Met. Station) – Whippendell Road – Pond Cross Roads – The Dome – Aldenham Road – Watford (High Street Garage). (STL)

355 St Albans (Lancaster Road) – Borehamwood. Certain journeys extended in Borehamwood from Red Lion to Potters Lane.

365 Luton – Hill End via Wheathampstead. One journey extended to Tyttenhanger.

393 Harlow (Green Man) – Hoddesdon. Extended in Hoddesdon to Middlefield Road.

426 Crawley – Charlwood – Horley – Crawley (circular). Shuttle service introduced across Crawley between Ifield (Bonnetts Lane) and Three Bridges.

437 Woking – Weybridge via Byfleet. Certain journeys extended in Weybridge from The Ship to Lincoln Arms.

445 Datchet Common – Windsor. Certain journeys extended to Old Windsor (Bells of Ouzeley) via Straight Road returning via Village Road.

In addition route 442 was seasonally extended to Burnham Beeches and route 474 re-introduced. Route 474 had operated on Whit Sunday and Monday. Route 376 was not extended to Whipsnade Zoo. The extension of route 308 to Cuffley, where it met route 242, provided a new interchange facility between the Central and Country areas. Route 309 garage journeys had traditionally been worked as route 321 between Leavesden Road Garage and Rickmansworth but from this date certain garage journeys ran over route 346 to Shrubs Corner.

On 4th July new route 325 was introduced between St Albans Garage and Cottonmill Estate to serve new council house development and was worked by just one STL. Route 370A was strengthened on the same date with increased frequency and a supplementary peak hour service was provided between Purfleet and Aveley (Foyle Drive). This was balanced by slight reductions on route 371.

The winter programme for 1951 was introduced on 26th September and saw the following revisions:

332 Cassiobury Park Estate – Oxhey Estate (Little Oxhey Lane). Intermediately re-routed away from Wood Waye and Green Lane to run via Brookdene Avenue.

338 Harperbury Hospital – St Albans with projections to Sandridge. Intermediately re-routed between Colney Cross Roads and London Colney via Bell Lane and Barnet Road vice route 358.

345 Kingswood – Northwood (Ducks Hill Road) via Wiggenhall Road with Monday to Saturday peak hour and Sunday afternoon projections to Harefield. Certain journeys from Kingswood re-routed to run via Brookdene Avenue to Oxhey Estate (Hayling Road).

346 Kingswood – Northwood (Ducks Hill Road) via Bushey Arches with Monday to Saturday peak hour and Sunday afternoon projections to Harefield. Certain journeys from Kingswood re-routed to run via Brookdene Avenue to Oxhey Estate (Hayling Road).

358 Borehamwood – St Albans via Shenley. Intermediately re-routed between Colney Cross Roads and London Colney via Napsbury Gates and Kings Road vice route 338.

394 Great Missenden – Chartridge – Chesham – Hyde Heath. Some journeys projected from Hyde Heath to Hyde End.

394C Amersham Garage – Hyde Heath (positioning journeys). Some journeys projected from Hyde Heath to Hyde End.

495 Northfleet – Kings Farm Estate via Waterdales and Parrock Street. Extended from Kings Farm Estate to Christianfields Estate. (Works journeys on route 495A were similarly extended on 5th February 1952).

Below: Route 308 was extended from Newgate Street to Cuffley on 13th June 1951 where connections could be made with Central Area route 242. TF 31 was displaced from Green Line work in 1952 and is seen climbing out of an undeveloped Cuffley. The destination blind is incorrectly set for route 308A. *Dilwyn Rees*

Below right: STL 2170 has been fitted with full blinds and is seen outside St Albans Garage working on route 354. The information content of the blinds is a vast improvement on STL 993 in the next photograph. *Ron Wellings*

Route 325 was introduced on 4th July 1951 to serve new housing development at Cottonmill Estate. In this December 1951 view RT 1014 and STL 993 stand side by side on St Albans Garage forecourt. *Alan B. Cross*

On 26th September 1951 route 338 was intermediately re-routed at London Colney to run via Bell Lane. Brand new RT 3450 is seen at St Albans Garage prior to working a journey on the route. *Alan B. Cross*

On 26th September 1951 an operating economy was made on route 387 when a 4Q4 was replaced by a 20-seat one-man operated vehicle. CR 17 is seen in Western Road, Tring in June 1952. Note the splendid double flag compulsory bus and coach stop. Some people preferred to cycle! *Alan B. Cross*

In order to meet the needs of the developing new town route 302 was extended from Hemel Hempstead town centre to Adeyfield on 20th February 1952. RT 612 stands at the Longlands terminus in the still developing area. The small black sticker in the top left hand corner of the stop flag denotes 'fare stage' and would have been applied as a result of the debacle following the March 1952 fares revision. *Omnibus Society*

In addition the seasonal withdrawals applied with route 313 no longer serving Whipsnade Zoo, route 442 no longer serving Burnham Beeches and the withdrawal of route 474. With route 338 it should be explained that Middlesex Colony had been redesignated Harperbury Hospital in April 1950. An operating economy was made on route 387 when a 4Q4 was replaced, daily, by a Cub. An additional 4Q4 continued to be used on Monday to Friday. It had been proposed to re-route the 318 in Croxley Green away from part of New Road and The Green to run via Barton Way, Sherbourne Way and Repton Way to Baldwins Lane to serve new housing. Rickmansworth Urban District Council favoured a service from the area to Rickmansworth and did not consider that the rerouteing of the 318 would fulfil residents' needs, thus it refused to make the highway improvements essential to the introduction of the service.

A minor alteration took place to High Wycombe local route 326 on 24th October 1951 when some journeys were extended in Micklefield Estate from Herbert Road to Buckingham Drive. On 2nd January 1952 short journeys on route 333 terminating at Bengeo House were amended to terminate at Parker Avenue. Route 376 Luton

– Kensworth gained a projection of one journey to Studham on 6th February.

Continuing housing development in the new towns accounted for some revisions to services on 20th February 1952:

302 Watford Heath – Hemel Hempstead (The Parade). Extended from The Parade to Adeyfield (Longlands).

320 Watford – Boxmoor Station. Intermediately re-routed away from Longlands to run via Adeyfield (Saracens Head) thus reverting to the pre 13th June 1951 routeing.

396 Epping – Bishop's Stortford. Shuttle service introduced from Harlow (Green Man) to Harlow New Town. (RT)

As a consequence of the revision to the 302, route 301C, which had interworked with route 302, was amended to run during the Monday to Friday off-peak period between Hemel Hempstead and Berkhamsted Station instead of Dudswell. Why the 396 shuttle service, which ran at right angles to the main route, was not given a separate number will forever remain a mystery. What was described as Harlow New Town was a point in an undeveloped sea of mud at the junction of First Avenue and an as yet un-named road designated "Road E".

The post-war condition of increasing costs of wages and increasing costs of fuel and raw materials were things that London Transport had not had to contend with before the war. The level of increase in fares asked for in October 1950 had not been fully sanctioned which meant that the increase had yielded about £1 million per year less than was required. The British Transport Commission was now seeking to increase fares on the main line railways and all London Transport services. Such proposals had to be submitted for approval to the Transport Tribunal, an independent body. By way of explanation the London Transport Executive produced a very carefully worded letter issued to staff in July 1951 explaining the need for a further fares increase. Across all LT services, including the Underground, the revision was expected to bring in an extra £8 million per year which the Executive maintained was necessary if it was to pay its way. The letter continued to explain that London Transport had a duty to provide an adequate service and to meet its costs. It was stated that working expenses had increased by 90 per cent since 1939 whereas fares had risen by only 43 per cent. The proposals, if accepted fully, would mean that the fares rose to 68 per cent above the 1939 level. The letter concluded that passengers were being asked to pay the costs of the services that they used, a situation that London Transport considered fair and reasonable.

The Transport Tribunal duly sanctioned what was officially termed the British Transport Commission (Passenger) Charges Scheme 1952. The increase applied on all LT services and the main line railways in the London area from 2nd March 1952. Main line rail fares outside London were to be revised at a later date. The ordinary fare scale for road services was 1½d per mile with fractions of 1d being charged as 1d with a minimum fare of 2d. In order to achieve this all routes had to be surveyed to obtain a distance of one mile for the new fare of 2d. This meant that many fare stages were altered and new ones inserted. By the implementation date all Central Bus, tram and trolleybus routes and the southern Country Area routes had been surveyed and the arrangements were reflected in the new fare-tables. The northern Country Area routes had not been surveyed and while the fare increases were applied, the stages remained largely unchanged. There were also increases in Early Morning Single fares, weekly tickets and the few surviving return fares. The usual exceptions applied where London Transport services observed other operators' fare scales. Minimum fares to enable priority to be given to long distance passengers applied on routes 406 and 418 ex Kingston and 450, 451, 489/A, 490/A and 492 ex Gravesend. Miniature fare-tables which had previously been introduced in the Central Area were now issued to Country Bus conductors and one-man drivers. As can be seen the increases in fares were severe:

Old fare	New fare	Old fare	New fare
1½d	2d	8d	9d
3d	3d	9d	11d
4d	5d	10d	1s 0d
5d	6d	11½d	1s 2d
6½d	8d		

and so on with a maximum fare of 3s 11d. In many cases, however, the new fare was higher as where an additional fare stage had been inserted, for example, a 4d fare might increase to 6d.

T 635 recently displaced from Green Line duties receives some attention from one of the Dunton Green engineers between trips on the 404 at Sevenoaks Bus Station. There is probably a difficulty with the steering as the front wheels have been jacked up off the ground despite the vehicle having a good load of passengers. *Alan B. Cross*

Route 330A linked Cole Green Lane in Welwyn Garden City with the factory area in Black Fan Road. RT 1045 stands at the Cole Green Lane terminus. Note the local advertisement for Welwyn Stores. Country Area buses carried a high proportion of local advertisements. *Alan B. Cross*

On 5th March 1952 route 312 was revised to run between Little Bushey and Cassiobury Park Estate. An immaculate RT 3461 had only been in service for just over a month when photographed passing its home garage of Watford High Street on 27th March 1952. *Alan B. Cross*

As might be expected public protest was both immediate and considerable with the press highlighting the matter. There were questions in the House of Commons which put the government in a somewhat delicate position. The British Transport Commission was the creation of the Attlee Labour administration which had been replaced in October 1951 by Churchill's Conservative administration. The government eventually decided that while the basic increase in fares was acceptable, the insertion of additional fare stages was not. Accordingly a further revision of fares, as far as the Country Area was concerned principally to the southern area routes, applied from 31st August 1952 when the fare stages reverted to the pre March 1952 position. The government directed that the travelling public should at least be advised as to the location of the fare stages. To this end small black paper stickers were applied to all bus stop flags at the fare stage points. This task commenced on 30th August in the Country Area and was completed within one week. The paper stickers were eventually superseded by the provision of designated e-plates and other enamel-iron fittings.

The LCC estate at Oxhey had been completed at the beginning of 1952 with a total of 4,333 new houses which led to a revision of services in the area on 5th March 1952 as follows:

312 Watford (Gammons Lane) – Little Bushey. Revised to run between Cassiobury Park Estate and Little Bushey replacing part of route 332.

332 Cassiobury Park Estate – Oxhey Estate (Little Oxhey Lane) route withdrawn.

345 Kingswood – Northwood (Ducks Hill Road) via Wiggenhall Road with Monday to Saturday peak hour and Sunday afternoon projections to Harefield – certain journeys from Kingswood to Oxhey Estate (Hayling Road). Completely revised to run from Watford (Chilcott Road) to Oxhey (Hillcroft Crescent) via Wiggenhall Road. No Sunday service.

346 Kingswood – Northwood (Ducks Hill Road) via Bushey Arches with Monday to Saturday peak hour and Sunday afternoon projections to Harefield – certain journeys from Kingswood to Oxhey Estate (Hayling Road). Completely revised to run from Kingswood to Oxhey Estate (Hallows Crescent) via Bushey Arches.

346A New route Kingswood to Oxhey Estate (Little Oxhey Lane) via Bushey Arches replacing part of routes 332 and 345.

347 New route Watford (Chilcott Road) – Northwood (Ducks Hill Road) via Bushey Arches with Monday to Saturday peak hour and Sunday afternoon projections to Harefield replacing part of routes 312, 345 and 346.

All of the above routes were RT worked.

The March 1952 service revision in Watford resulted in a new route 346A from Oxhey Estate, Little Oxhey Lane to Kingswood. RT 1035 with cream upper deck window surrounds and full blinds loads up at the combined bus and coach compulsory stop at Watford Market Place. Note the 'Q' plate below the stop flag. *LTPS/D.A. Jones*

Brand new RT 3462 undergoes a crew change outside Watford High Street Garage while working on newly introduced route 347 in March 1952. Note the conductor's metal carrying case for his tickets and Bell Punch machine – rather larger than those provided for Gibson machines. *Alan B. Cross*

Hatfield's RT 1097 is seen at the White Lion on Stevenage local route 392 which was introduced on 26th March 1952. The bus was initially outstationed in Julians Road, Stevenage but the arrangements proved unsatisfactory. T 621 is seen behind working a short journey to Walkern on route 384. *Alan B. Cross*

The needs of the expanding new towns were destined to have a major effect in the provision of bus services over the years. Two changes were introduced on 26th March 1952. Route 330 was re-routed away from a section of the Barnet By-Pass at New Hatfield to run via Birchwood Avenue and Longmead to rejoin the line of route at Oldings Corner. Route 392 ran from Stevenage (White Lion) to Monks Wood via Haycroft Road, Greydells Road, Poppleway and Six Hills Way to Monks Wood Way. Hitchin Garage could not accommodate double deckers on account of the height of the roof so the one RT needed was provided by Hatfield and out-stationed at Stevenage in a yard in Julians Road. The operation required two crews and arrangements were made with the engineering department to refuel the bus locally. Ticket boxes were provided to the conductors weekly by an official from Hitchin Garage and arrangements were made with the British Railways for conductors to pay in their takings at Stevenage Station booking office. The arrangements clearly proved to be less than satisfactory and in May the crews were deemed to be part of the staffing establishment at

Hitchin Garage pending the further augmentation of services in Stevenage. Incredibly the route terminated at the White Lion, 0.39 miles short of the railway station, which led to complaints from British Railways, the local authority and residents. Matters were corrected on 24th September 1952 when route 392 was revised to run from Stevenage Station to Monks Wood via Sish Lane direct instead of Haycroft Road and Greydells Road. New route 392A ran from Stevenage Station to Bedwell via Haycroft Road, Greydells Road, Poppleway and Bedwell Crescent. One journey each way on Monday to Friday on route 392A ran to Monks Wood for school requirements. Both routes were worked by RTs from Hitchin and as far as can be established the out-stationing ceased at or before this date. A yard was acquired at Hitchin to accommodate double-deck vehicles and eventually the garage roof was jacked up to allow double deckers to enter for maintenance purposes. It should be noted that the Stevenage Station referred to was sited approximately one mile north of the present station which was opened on 23rd July 1973.

Enhanced services to Aveley LCC Estate were provided on 30th April 1952 when the following alterations applied:

315 New route of works journeys formerly provided by route 328A between Woodside Estate and Purfleet Station.

328 Ockendon Station – Aveley – Stonehouse Corner – Grays – Woodside Estate and works journeys Ockendon Station – Purfleet Station. Revised to run between Aveley LCC Estate (Elan Road) and Woodside Estate via Foyle Drive, North Stifford and Grays.

328A Purfleet Station – Stonehouse Corner – Grays – Woodside Estate (works journeys). Revised to provide works journeys from Purfleet Station to Aveley LCC Estate (Elan Road) and a daily shuttle service from Aveley (Hall Road) to Aveley LCC Estate (Elan Road) via Foyle Drive. Buses connected at Elan Road with route 328 to provide a link to Grays.

328B New route providing works journeys from Purfleet Station to Ockendon Station replacing a section of route 328.

All of the above routes were allocated RTs, supplemented by one STL on Monday to Friday. Route 328 now provided a direct link between Aveley LCC Estate and Grays rather than by running via Stonehouse Corner. In addition works service 368 from Grays to Bata Shoe Factory now had journeys re-routed to operate via Hathaway Road and Lodge Lane.

New route 328B was introduced on 30th April 1952 to provide a works service between Ockendon Station and Purfleet Station. RT 3503 is seen in Aveley Village with passengers keen to alight. *Alan B. Cross*

The needs of the developing LCC estate at Aveley were responsible for a number of service revisions in the Grays area. On 30th April 1952 a new route 315 replaced part of route 328A to provide works journeys between Purfleet Station and Woodside Estate. RT 1061 is seen in Grays town centre. *Alan B. Cross*

On 21st May 1952 part of the service on route 325 was extended during Monday to Friday peak hours and Saturday shopping hours from St Albans Garage to Townsend. RT 3523 has been parked out of service in Grange Street, opposite the side entrance of the garage.
Alan B. Cross

In advance of the summer programme for 1952, on 14th May new route 420 was introduced between Woking and Sheerwater LCC Estate worked by just one STL from Addlestone Garage. In addition, route 461A (Walton – Ottershaw with projections to Botleys Park (St Peter's Hospital) on Wednesday and Sunday) saw the Botleys Park projections extended to Holloway Hill daily. On 21st May route 313 was seasonally reinstated to Whipsnade Zoo and St Albans local route 325 (St Albans Garage to Cottonmill Estate) was revised to provide a cross-city service between Townsend and Cottonmill Estate.

Garage facilities in Watford had been stretched since before the war and despite the withdrawal of Green Line coaches from Leavesden Road, the expansion of works services and routes to serve new housing had exacerbated the problem. A yard opposite Watford High Street Garage had been acquired in 1942 and in the post-war period approximately 40 vehicles were parked there overnight. It was fifteen years since a new Country Area garage had been built and advances in design had been considerable. A site for the new garage was acquired in St Albans Road at Garston and the opening was planned for June 1952. The two-storey administrative

block and canteen fronted the main road and were separated from the main building by a forecourt for the use of terminating buses. The docking unit abutted the main running shed and as much glazing as possible was used in the construction in order to facilitate natural lighting. The garage was designed to accommodate 150 buses but the initial allocation was 69. The excess capacity was to house expansion, especially in connection with new town development which in the event largely never came. Leavesden Road Garage was closed and its buses transferred to Garston together with routes 301A, 321, the 344 group, 347 and 351 from Watford High Street where the yard opposite was no longer required. Watford High Street's allocation dropped from 83 buses to 45. Proposals to close Watford High Street Garage completely at the time had also been considered but as a number of routes did not pass the new garage it was estimated that some 13 extra crew duties would be required. As the Watford garages had a higher than average staff shortage this proposal was not adopted. Garston was due to open on 11th June to coincide with the summer programme but the opening was, in fact, deferred until 18th June.

With the opening of Garston Garage on 18th June 1952 some of the Watford High Street routes were transferred which meant that the High Street's allocation dropped by 38 buses. As a result of this change an overspill yard opposite which had been used since 1942 was no longer required. Chiswick bodied front entrance STL 1007 dating from 1935 is parked up in the yard between trips on works route 301A. *F.G. Reynolds*

With the opening of Garston Garage the 344 group of works services were transferred from Watford High Street to the new garage. An immaculate RT 4194 is seen turning into its home garage before the change. *Alan B. Cross*

On 11th June 1952 certain journeys on route 434 between Horsham and Edenbridge were renumbered 473 and ran via Rowfant instead of Copthorne. T 792, a 15T13 type now privately preserved, is seen working the service. *John Herting collection*

Two new routes, 473 and 498 were introduced on 11th June. Route 473 consisted of alternate Monday to Saturday journeys formerly provided by route 434 between Horsham and Edenbridge which were re-routed between Three Bridges and Turners Hill to run via Rowfant instead of Copthorne and was worked by T type single-deckers. In Gravesend part of the 497 service between the Clock Tower and Dover Road Schools was run as 498 from Clock Tower to Coldharbour Estate using STLs. In addition route 442 was seasonally extended to Burnham Beeches on Monday to Saturday and Sunday route 474 was re-introduced although the latter had run at Whitsun on 1st and 2nd June.

The following route changes applied on 18th June with the opening of Garston Garage:

316   Chesham – Adeyfield. Intermediately re-routed between Hemel Hempstead and Boxmoor to run via Station Road, St John's Road and Fishery Road instead of Two Waters.

318C   Kings Langley Station – Two Waters via Ovaltine Works and Apsley Mills (journeys only). Journeys provided from Watford (Clarendon Corner) via Garston and Abbots Langley in that direction only.

320   Boxmoor – Hemel Hempstead – Adeyfield – Watford withdrawn, replaced by route 347.

335   Windsor – Watford (Leavesden Road Garage). Revised to terminate at Watford High Street Garage.

336   Chesham – Watford (Leavesden Road Garage). Revised to terminate at Watford High Street Garage.

344   Watford Met. Station – Brockley Hill via Whippendell Road, Pond Cross Roads, The Dome and Watford By-Pass (works journeys). Certain positioning journeys run to and from Garston Garage.

344A   Watford Met. Station – Brockley Hill via Whippendell Road, Watford Junction, The Dome and Watford By-Pass (works journeys). Certain positioning journeys run to and from Garston Garage.

344B   Watford Met. Station – Whippendell Road – Pond Cross Roads – The Dome – Aldenham Road – Watford High Street Garage (works journeys in this direction only). Projected from High Street Garage to Market Place.

345   Watford (Chilcott Road) – Oxhey (Hillcroft Crescent) via Wiggenhall Road. Revised to run from North Watford (Maytree Crescent) to Oxhey (Hillcroft Crescent) via Wiggenhall Road. Some early journeys to Chilcott Road retained and some early journeys routed via Bushey Arches instead of Wiggenhall Road.

347   Watford (Chilcott Road) – Northwood (Ducks Hill Road) via Bushey Arches with Monday to Saturday peak hour and Sunday afternoon projections to Harefield. Revised to start from Boxmoor Station via Adeyfield replacing route 320, section to Chilcott Road withdrawn.

Route 316 had been re-routed to run via Two Waters in 1944 to facilitate ST operation. Although the route was converted from ST to T operation in September 1950 it was not until now that the traditional routeing via Boxmoor was resumed.

With the opening of Garston Garage on 18th June 1952 a major revision of services in the area took place. Route 320 from Watford to Boxmoor was replaced by revised route 347. Two Waters based T 786 is seen heading for Watford through undeveloped countryside. *Ron Wellings*

A minor adjustment was made to route 311 from 6th August 1952 when one late evening journey was extended from Chilcott Road to Leavesden (Ganders Ash) over route 306. Route 313 lost its seasonal extension to Whipsnade from 24th September and route 358 short workings to Napsbury Lane (North Cottages) were withdrawn. The full winter programme applied in the North and North East Districts from 8th October when route 382 lost the projections to Sandridge and was revised to run between St Albans Garage and Codicote. The winter programme came in on 15th October 1952 across the rest of the network when the following changes applied:

345 North Watford (Maytree Crescent) to Oxhey (Hillcroft Crescent) via Wiggenhall Road. Some early journeys to Chilcott Road and some early journeys routed via Bushey Arches instead of Wiggenhall Road. Entire service routed via Bushey Arches.

351 Harpenden – Uxbridge. One Monday to Friday evening peak journey from the Watford direction projected from Rickmansworth to Chorleywood (The Gate) to supplement routes 335 and 336.

373 Penn – Beaconsfield – Holtspur. Withdrawn between Beaconsfield and Holtspur.

398 Amersham – Beaconsfield via Coleshill with a projection to Holtspur. Holtspur projection withdrawn.

419 Langley Vale – Epsom – West Ewell. Withdrawn between West Ewell and Epsom (Brettgrave), section adequately covered by route 418.

420 Woking – Sheerwater (LCC Estate). Extended from Sheerwater to West Byfleet Station. Monday to Saturday peak hours and garage journeys to and from Addlestone now run in service.

438 East Grinstead – Crawley (works service). Journey to Crawley Down provided.

463A New route Walton – Ripley (Sunday pm only) replacing some journeys on route 436A. (RLH)

STL 2682, the first of the 18STL20 batch dating from 1946 and in all over green livery attracts little custom from a crowded Watford High Street on its journey to Watford Met. Station.
Alan B. Cross

Above left: Route 455B between Beaconsfield and Cliveden Hospital was withdrawn after 26th October 1952. High Wycombe's RT 3198 is seen at the garage after working the route. *Alan B. Cross*

Above right: On 5th November 1952 a number of service reductions were made in Grays. London Transport obviously considered the service levels that it had inherited from Eastern National to be too generous. The service on route 323A was halved and in this view STL 670 attracts no custom. Having spent most of its life in central area service, the bus was painted into green livery as late as November 1951. *Alan B. Cross*

This was the last summer season when route 442 was extended from Farnham Royal to Burnham Beeches. The Sunday only route 474 was seasonally withdrawn for the winter. The unserved section of route 345 via Wiggenhall Road, which had seen a bus service since the 1920s, caused public complaints to London Transport but it maintained that adequate services were available within a reasonable walking distance. Routes 373 and 398 had certain Holtspur journeys reinstated for school children on Monday to Friday from 21st January 1953.

Route 328C was introduced on 5th November 1952 to provide the residents of Aveley Estate with a direct link to Rainham. T 794 loads up at Rainham Clock Tower. *LTPS/D.A. Jones*

In October 1952 the 333B terminus at Ware Park Sanatorium was redesignated Ware Park Hospital and route 455B (Beaconsfield – Cliveden Hospital) was withdrawn, running for the last time on 26th October 1952. A number of adjustments to timetables were made in the Grays area on 5th November with journeys being cut on routes 315, 371 and 371A while the main service on route 323A between Grays and Nutberry Corner was effectively halved. On route 323B one of the morning projections to Purfleet was further extended to Tank Hill returning as route 323A. Residents of the LCC estate at Aveley had complained about the lack of a direct link to Rainham and the matter was redressed with the introduction of route 328C running Monday to Friday peak hours only between Elan Road and Rainham via Aveley High Street, Purfleet Road and Wennington. On the same date Monday to Friday works journeys were provided on route 405 between Manor Royal and Three Bridges Station. On 12th November certain Monday to Friday peak hour journeys on routes 301C, 302 and 316 were projected to Maylands Avenue in Hemel Hempstead in order to serve the new industrial area. Changes in St Albans on 3rd December saw route 325 extended in Townsend from Batchworth View to Connaught Road and route 391A was extended from Townsend (Connaught Road) to New Greens Estate (Woollam Crescent) in order to serve new housing. Also on 3rd December approximately half of the 477 service terminating in Dartford at Temple Hill Estate (now designated St Vincents Road) was re-routed at the town centre via Temple Hill and Littlebrook Manor Way to terminate at the junction with Henderson Drive. Housing development in the new town meant the introduction of RT worked route 314A from Bennetts End (Peascroft Road) to Hemel Hempstead (The Parade) on 17th December. New route 330B was introduced on 31st December 1952 to provide Monday to Friday journeys between St Albans Garage and Hatfield Technical College which was located in Roe Green Lane.

Top: On 5th November 1952 a supplementary service was introduced on route 405 from Three Bridges Station to the developing industrial area at Manor Royal in Crawley. The garage at Crawley was small and as the services for the new town expanded most buses had to be parked in the open. In this view STL 1729, which has worked a journey on works route 438 from East Grinstead, stands next to RT 3676 which has worked on the 405 supplementary service. *LCC Tramway Trust/ D. Battams*

Centre: On 12th November 1952 St Albans local route 391A was extended from Townsend to serve new housing at New Greens Estate. Q 83 is seen in St Peters Street working on the route prior to the extension. The roof board brackets indicate that the vehicle was one of 27 4Q4 Country Buses temporarily upgraded to Green Line status in 1937. The vehicle is now preserved. *LTPS/D.A. Jones*

Right: New route 314A was introduced on 17th December 1952 to run from Hemel Hempstead Parade to the newly developing area, Bennetts End. Smartly turned out RT 622 is seen working on the route. *Alan B. Cross*

RT 3886 stands in rural surroundings at Holmer Green prior to returning to High Wycombe on a short journey on route 362.
C. Carter

An additional facility for Oxhey Estate was provided on 7th January 1953 when route 346B ran between the 346 terminus at Hallowes Crescent and the 346A terminus at Little Oxhey Lane during Monday to Friday peak hours primarily to provide a feeder service to Carpenders Park Station. One RT from Watford High Street Garage was required. On 14th January in response to much public complaint some journeys on route 347 terminating at Northwood (Ducks Hill Road) were extended the short distance to Mount Vernon Hospital at certain times. On 28th January some journeys on route 424 at Stone Quarry Estate in East Grinstead were re-routed to Blackwell County Primary School.

The shuttle service on route 396 was, as far as can be established, renumbered 396A on 21st January 1953, withdrawn between Harlow (Green Man) and Harlow (Post Office) and extended further along First Avenue to Halling Hill. Certain journeys ran through from Halling Hill to either Epping or Bishop's Stortford over

route 396. Route 393 was revised to have some journeys terminate at Harlow (Post Office) instead of Green Man on the same date. The 396A changes had been deferred from 24th September 1952. On 4th February 1953 journeys on route 478 (Swanley – Wrotham) were extended in Swanley from Station North Side to St Mary's Estate.

In 1953 a number of services for the convenience of hospital visitors were introduced with the buses picking up at defined points and conveying passengers only to and from the hospital concerned. The first to be introduced was route 482 from Caterham Station to Smallfield Hospital via Godstone, Bletchingley and Redhill on 1st March using one RT from Godstone. Initially only a Sunday service was provided but a Thursday service commenced on 11th June by local arrangement and officially one week later. The second such service, route 493, commenced on 12th April running on Sunday afternoon from Englefield Green (Larchwood Drive) to Botleys Park (St Peters Hospital) via Egham, Stroude,

Christchurch Cross Roads and Thorpe. One RT from Staines was used. Route 472 from Leatherhead Garage to Netherne Hospital near Coulsdon via Epsom, Sutton, Carshalton and Wallington commenced on Sunday 19th April. One week later the RT which worked the route provided a shuttle service between Netherne Hospital entrance and the main gate on the Brighton Road where connections were available with routes 405 and 414. A Wednesday service was also provided from 29th April. On 28th June route 345 commenced between Watford High Street Garage and Napsbury Hospital via Watford Junction, North Watford, Garston and North Orbital Road. The route was operated initially only on Sunday but a Wednesday journey was added from 14th July 1954.

Various minor adjustments applied on 4th March 1953 when routes 315 and 328 were extended in Woodside Estate from Grangewood Road to Buxton Avenue. On route 342 a short journey from Hertford to Broxbourne Station was extended over route 327 to Nazeing Gate for school children. Routes 405, 434 and 473 works journeys were further extended in Crawley along Manor Royal to Faraday Road. Also in Crawley certain journeys on the 426 Ifield – Three Bridges shuttle service were re-routed away from a section of Ifield Road to run via Ewhurst Road and West Green Drive.

Central Area buses were often loaned to Country Area garages at summer weekends and bank holidays where they allowed green buses to be used on Green Line relief duties. Red RT 1746 has been loaned to Swanley and is seen on route 478. *M.G. Webber*

A number of limited stop services for the use of hospital visitors were introduced in 1953. The first one was 482 on 1st March which linked Caterham Station with Smallfield Hospital. Godstone's RT 3454 waits outside the station. *Alan B. Cross*

Below: RTC I was a one-off vehicle which was used at Leatherhead mostly on routes 416 and 468 between December 1949 and March 1953. The vehicle started life as RT 97 but following bomb damage had been rebuilt as an experimental pay as you board vehicle and then as experimental Green Line coach RTC I entering service in April 1949. It was not successful in Green Line service and was relegated to bus work at Leatherhead. RTC I is seen in this view in Esher on route 416.
Alan B. Cross

Bottom: Long established route 309 from Rickmansworth to Uxbridge was curtailed to run between Rickmansworth and Harefield on 6th May 1953 when RT operated route 347 was extended from Harefield to Uxbridge. T 790 in all over green livery is seen at Uxbridge Station departing for Rickmansworth in July 1952.
Alan B. Cross

London Transport was aware of the need to provide new and enhanced garage facilities in areas where services were planned to expand to meet the needs of new housing and a statement dated 2nd April 1953 set out proposals for Country Buses and Coaches as shown in the table below:

The figures include Green Line coaches and the present allocation figures include engineering spares. Capacity figures include vehicles parked in the open. The proposed requirements proved to be extremely optimistic and the actual figures never reached such levels. In the event new garages opened at Hatfield and Stevenage in 1959 and Harlow in 1963 but new premises at Crawley were eventually built by London Country. The building of a new garage at Slough would have saved much unproductive running to and from Windsor. There had been a proposal in 1946 with the re-establishment of Green Line services to re-open the Slough Langley Road premises but the plan was never implemented.

Garage	Present capacity	Present allocation	Post 1957 proposed	Remarks
Epping	44	41	96	New garage at Harlow 1958 future requirement 150
Hitchin	18	21	62	New garage at Stevenage 1958 future requirement 75
Hatfield	34	32	60	New garage 1957/8
Two Waters	70	54	80	Consideration deferred
Windsor	100	92	141	New garage at Slough urgently required
Crawley	39	28	47	New garage 1957/8
Grays	102	96	112	Consideration deferred

The summer programme for 1953 which commenced on 6th May involved revised timetables for most routes and the following alterations:

309   Rickmansworth – Uxbridge with peak hour journeys from Harefield West to Uxbridge. Revised to run between Rickmansworth and Harefield (Truesdale Drive) and withdrawn from Harefield West (see route 347).

313   Enfield – St Albans. Seasonally extended to Whipsnade Zoo.

318D   New school route Watford (Clarendon Corner) – Langleybury School via Garston and Abbots Langley. One journey returning from Langleybury School is projected from Watford to Sarratt. (T)

324   New route Aveley LCC Estate (Eskley Gardens) – Grays via Daiglen Drive, North Stifford and Nutberry Corner. Some journeys and part of Sunday service extended from Grays to Woodside Estate (Buxton Road). (RT)

325   Townsend (Connaught Road) – Cottonmill Estate (Wallingford Walk). Slight extension in Cottonmill Estate to Abbots Avenue.

328   Aveley LCC Estate (Elan Road) – Woodside Estate via Foyle Drive, North Stifford and Grays. Terminus changed from Elan Road to Humber Avenue.

328A   Aveley (Hall Road) – Aveley LCC Estate (Elan Road) daily shuttle service and Purfleet Station – Aveley LCC Estate (Elan Road) works journeys. Route withdrawn (see 332).

332   New route Aveley (Hall Road) – Aveley LCC Estate (Eskley Gardens) via Foyle Drive, Darenth Drive and Daiglen Drive also works journeys Purfleet Stn – Eskley Gardens. (RT)

334   New works route Two Waters Garage – Hemel Hempstead (Maylands Avenue) via Durrants Hill Road, Barnacres Road and Bennetts End Road. (RT)

345   North Watford (Maytree Crescent) – Oxhey (Hillcroft Crescent) via Bushey Arches with certain early journeys to Chilcott Road route

withdrawn. Increased service provided on 347 to Hillcroft Crescent.

346A Kingswood – Oxhey Estate (Little Oxhey Lane) via Bushey Arches. Extended from Little Oxhey Lane to Heysham Drive.

347 Boxmoor Station – Northwood (Ducks Hill Road) via Bushey Arches with Monday to Saturday peak hour and Sunday afternoon projections to Harefield. Revised to run daily between Boxmoor Station and Uxbridge replacing route 309 between Harefield and Uxbridge. Peak hour journeys from Harefield West to Uxbridge also provided ex 309.

369 Sandridge – Dunstable (Square) with works projections to AC Delco Works. Two am peak journeys re-routed from St Albans to Sandridgebury School via Harpenden Road on schooldays only.

374 Grays – Uplands Estate – Aveley (Tunnel Garage) with projections to Rainham. Limited Sunday service provided from Tilbury (Feenan Highway) – Uplands Estate via Dock Road and Grays.

435 Leatherhead – Tadworth (hospital journeys Stoke D'Abernon – Leatherhead). Intermediately re-routed between Leatherhead and Headley to serve Headley Court RAF Hospital.

438A East Grinstead (Bus Station) – Crawley (George) via Snow Hill, Copthorne, Tinsley Green and Lowfield Heath (works journeys). Intermediately re-routed between Copthorne and Tinsley Green away from Shipley Bridge via Ridleys Corner to facilitate double-deck working. Converted from T to STL operation.

447 Redhill – Doods Road – Reigate – Earlswood – Redhill – South Merstham and Reigate – Earlswood – Redhill – South Merstham – Woldingham (two sections). Most of South Merstham terminating service extended to serve new LCC estate terminating at Merstham (Delabole Road).

474 Slough Station – Burnham Beeches via Bath Road, Sunday only. Re-introduced for summer.

481 New route Epsom (Clock Tower) – Epsom (Wells Estate). (C)

483 New route Crawley (George) – Northgate (Midgeley Road). (STL)

The original proposal for a service to the LCC Estate at Merstham had been to extend route 430 (Reigate – South Park – Redhill) from Redhill. Route 430 was RT worked but two low railway bridges in Battlebridge Road would have meant conversion to RLH. This was approved by the traffic commissioner subject to road improvements and the introduction of traffic light control under one of the bridges. Presumably problems with the local authority resulted in the alternative extension of the single-deck operated route 447 South Merstham journeys.

Route 347 was extended from Harefield to Uxbridge on 6th May 1953 in order to provide double-deck capacity over that section. RT 4175 heading for Uxbridge takes on passengers at Garston Garage. *Omnibus Society*

Epsom local route 481 was introduced on 6th May 1953. CR 43 is seen at Epsom Station.

Route 483 was introduced on 6th May 1953 to link Crawley with Northgate. With a great deal of building work in progress in the new towns the roads were often muddy and the buses frequently became mud spattered. STL 1011 stands at a temporary stop sign at the, as yet, undeveloped Northgate terminus. As a result of war damage and body rebuilding STL 1011 was one of the front entrance vehicles to be fitted with a surplus roof box body in 1947/8. *Alan B. Cross/Prince Marshall*

On 6th May 1953 part of the service on route 447 was extended to the new Merstham LCC Estate. RF 650 loads up outside the new London Transport enquiry office and waiting room at Redhill. *London Transport Museum*

Watford High Street based RT 3648 shows the publicity displayed over the Coronation period. *London Transport Museum*

Coronation Day, Tuesday 2nd June 1953, was a public holiday and an enhanced Sunday service was provided on Country Buses. In a number of instances the services started between 3am and 4am in order to provide connections with early Green Line coaches and trains to London for those wishing to view the procession. A series of evening excursions operated between 3rd and 21st June from 18 destinations in the Country Area mostly using RTs to view the Coronation route and various floodlit buildings.

A minor adjustment was made to route 358 (St Albans – Borehamwood via Napsbury Gates and Shenley) from 25th July 1953 when a supplementary service was introduced on Saturday between St Albans and Sheep House Farm Estate at London Colney.

A further revision of fares applied on all London Transport services from 16th August 1953. As far as buses were concerned the 2d minimum and 5d remained unchanged, the 3d and 8d fares were increased by ½d and all other fares were increased by 1d. Non-standard fares applied on a number of routes due the influence of other operators' fare scales which were not subject of revision at the time. Early morning single fares were in some cases increased costing between 3d and 10d according to the distance travelled. The monthly return fare between Aylesbury and Wendover on route 359 which was jointly worked with United Counties was withdrawn at this time. The only remaining return fares were now two day-return bookings on route 339 over the Ongar to Brentwood section where Eastern National fare scales applied. Weekly tickets in some parts of the Northern Area continued to be available at nine times the single fare subject to a minimum of 7d and, exceptionally, in some cases 6d.

Traditionally the ticket issuing method used was the Bell Punch system, the origins of which dated back to the 1890s. The cost of printing, storing, and distributing tickets and replenishing ticket boxes was high with the system requiring strict audit controls. Both the LGOC and London Transport had conducted experiments with various forms of mechanisation beginning in the 1920s. Where a return journey or transfer facility applied London Transport felt it desirable that the geographical points were shown on the ticket which ruled out mechanisation on the routes concerned. With the gradual simplification of fare structures mechanisation became a viable proposition. The superintendent of London Transport's ticket machine works, Mr George Gibson, developed what would be designated the Gibson ticket machine as a solution. The Gibson machine was capable of issuing 14 different values of ticket and recording the numbers sold for each fare value. Following experiments, the production batch of Gibson machines began to be introduced across London Transport's road services in 1953 with the first Country Area machines going to Garston for use on 27th September 1953. The whole network was gradually equipped and the last three Country Area garages to retain the Bell Punch system, Crawley, Dorking and Reigate were converted to Gibson operation on 17th November 1957. It should be noted that the range of the 14 different values was not consistent across the network as at certain garages the needs of other operators' fare scales were taken into account.

Conductress Mrs Phyllis White of Windsor Garage is wearing an Effra Road type ticket punch on a leather backplate fixed to her uniform jacket by screw-in type buttons. Note the griffins on the lapels and also on the metal buttons. The PSV badge has been issued by the South Eastern Traffic Commissioner – staff had to apply to the Traffic Commissioner in whose area they resided, not where their employer was based. *London Transport Museum*

Gibson ticket machines started to replace punch tickets in the Country Area in 1953. In this view taken at London Transport's Stockwell works a batch of machines for Watford High Street Garage are tested ready for use. *London Transport Museum*

305 Gerrards Cross – High Wycombe via The Chalfonts, Beaconsfield certain short journeys between Gerrards Cross and Chalfont St Peter. Re-routed via south-west and north sides of Gold Hill Common to serve Leachcroft Estate.

305A Gerrards Cross – Chalfont Common. Certain journeys re-routed via south-west and north sides of Gold Hill Common to serve Leachcroft Estate.

321A New route Luton – Rickmansworth (Berry Lane Estate). Utilising certain journeys on route 321 formerly terminating at Rickmansworth Met. Station or Maple Cross. (RT)

325 Townsend (Connaught Road) – Cottonmill Estate (Abbots Avenue). Extended in Townsend to junction of Batchwood Drive and Becketts Avenue and intermediately re-routed via Waverley Road, Everlasting Lane and Batchworth Drive.

346B Oxhey Estate local Hallowes Crescent – Little Oxhey Lane. Extended from the latter point to Heysham Drive (route 346A had been similarly extended on 6th May 1953).

348 Chesham Moor – Buckland Common or St Leonards. Short journeys provided between Chesham Broadway and Pond Park Estate (such journeys were designated 348A on 19th May 1954).

355 St Albans (Lancaster Road) – Borehamwood (Red Lion or Potters Lane). All journeys revised to terminate in Borehamwood at Cowley Hill.

396 Epping – Bishop's Stortford. Works journeys provided from Epping to Harlow New Town (Edinburgh Way) via First Avenue, Howard Way (yet to be named) and Edinburgh Way.

New housing development continued to provide extra traffic for Country Buses and on 5th August 1953, routes 436 (Staines – Guildford) and 436A (Staines – Ripley) were intermediately re-routed to serve Sheerwater LCC Estate near Woking. The winter timetables were introduced on 7th October 1953 and involved the following route alterations:

A supplementary service across Crawley from Ifield to Three Bridges on route 426 was introduced on 13th June 1951 and on 7th October 1953 the route was converted to RT operation. These two views at Crawley show T 787 working the service and the new order is represented by RT 3726. *LCC Tramway Trust/ D. Battams, Ron Wellings*

396A Harlow (Post Office) – Halling Hill. Further extended along First Avenue to The Dashes.

405 West Croydon – Crawley (George) with works projections to Manor Royal and Three Bridges. Monday to Friday projections to Crawley (Goffs Park) now provided.

423A Dartford – Joyce Green – Wells Factory (hospital and works journeys).
Re-routed away from a section of Joyce Green Lane to run via Trevithick Drive.

426 Crawley Circular via Charlwood and Horley and shuttle service Ifield (Bonnetts Lane) – Three Bridges. Shuttle service re-routed away from a section of Three Bridges Road to run via Mitchells Road, Gales Drive and North Road and converted from T to RT operation.

438 East Grinstead (Bus Station) – Crawley (works service). Withdrawn between East Grinstead and Crawley Down.

438A East Grinstead (Bus Station) – Crawley (George) via Snow Hill, Copthorne, Ridleys Corner, Tinsley Green and Lowfield Heath (works journeys). Journeys via Crawley Down provided vice 438.

477 Chelsfield (Saturday and Sunday) – Orpington (Kelvin Parade or Goddington Lane) – Dartford (St Vincents Road) or Littlebrook Manor Way. Section to St Vincents Road withdrawn – see routes 477A and 499. Works journeys projected to Littlebrook Power Station.

477A New route Chelsfield (Saturday and Sunday) or Orpington (Kelvin Parade or Goddington Lane) – Dartford (Joyce Green Lane, Trevithick Drive); former 477 St Vincents Road journeys renumbered and re-routed in Dartford. (RT)

499 New route Dartford Garage – St Vincents Road via East Hill. (RT)

In addition route 313 was seasonally withdrawn from Whipsnade Zoo and route 474 was seasonally withdrawn. Some minor alterations took place during November. Route 467 Sidcup – Horton Kirby or Wilmington via Dartford was re-routed away from Shepherds Lane on 11th November to run via Heath Lane and Highfield Road. On 18th November route 330B St Albans Garage – Hatfield Technical College had a journey projected in St Albans to Marshalswick. In addition new RT worked route 340A was introduced between Potters Bar and Hatfield Garage to serve Hatfield Technical College via Brookmans Park, Welham Green, Barnet By-Pass and St Albans Road. Route 367 Tilbury Docks – East Tilbury (Bata Shoe Factory) had some journeys intermediately re-routed via New Road and River View. On 25th November the projections on route 477 to Littlebrook Power Station were withdrawn.

On 7th October 1953 route 477 was revised to run from Chelsfield or Orpington to Dartford Littlebrook Manor Way with journeys running to Trevithick Drive in Dartford numbered 477A. In this view of RT 3598 at Orpington Station the route number 477 is displayed despite the destination. *Alan B. Cross*

CHAPTER 2 THE FLEET

At the start of 1950 there were 117 front entrance STLs in service, excluding the lowbridge type. STL 1025 was one of the original Chiswick bodied batch of 89 new in 1935. The seating capacity of only 48 had been increased to 52 during the early stages of the war. The Chiswick authorities over-ruled Mr. Hawkins, the Operating Manager, over the fitting of doors. STL 1025 stands in Dorking Bus Station between trips on route 429. *D.C. Fisk*

London Transport had decided that the RT would become the standard double-deck vehicle and, with the exception of the low-height fleet, would ultimately replace all existing LT, ST, STL and Utility types. The RTs delivered in 1948 and 1949 had replaced most of the STs and made small inroads in replacing the STLs. At the beginning of 1950, disregarding low-height buses, there were 319 green rear entrance STLs and 117 of the front entrance type in stock. Deliveries of RTs to the Country Area recommenced in February 1950 and followed on virtually continuously until October of that year ranging from RT 2116 to RT 3901 which was by no means a continuous sequence as the majority were Central Area buses.

The deliveries of new RTs allowed the withdrawal of many of the front entrance STLs. From February 1950 RTs were allocated to Chelsham and Dunton Green for the 403 group of routes, Crawley for 405, Reigate for 405 and 414 and Dorking for the 414. In April a further batch of buses went to East Grinstead, Godstone and Reigate for routes 409 and 411. This batch, from

Weymann, commenced with RT 3115 which was the first to appear in all over Lincoln green livery with just a cream band between the decks, the cream upper deck window surrounds having been dispensed with. This set a new standard for all subsequent deliveries. Further new buses went to Chelsham, Guildford and Leatherhead for the 408 and 470, Amersham and High Wycombe for the 362 group and 455 and Staines for the 441. The appearance of green RTs was further enhanced from RT 3137 onwards which were fitted with full blinds at Godstone, thus replacing the war-time economy of reducing the front via box area and painting other front boxes over. Blinds now appeared in all seven boxes of the RT. All earlier RTs would be so fitted over the next few years. A further batch of Weymann bodied buses commencing at RT 3857 were delivered in September and October 1950 to Windsor for the 441, Swanley for the 401, Dunton Green for the 402, Watford High Street and Windsor for the 335, Amersham for the 353 and Watford Leavesden Road for the 385.

STL 1029 was one of seven of the original batch of front entrance vehicles to be rebodied with rear entrance bodies in 1947/48. It is seen at Much Hadham on route 350 working from Hertford Garage.

Below left: A further batch of 50 front entrance STLs with bodies built by Weymann were delivered in 1936. The bodies contained a number of detail differences from the Chiswick built ones, most noticeably the position of the front destination box above the route number and intermediate points box. They remained as 48 seaters throughout their working lives which caused problems as to which routes they could be allocated at this period. STL 1472 is seen at Sevenoaks Bus Station on route 431 in August 1950; it was withdrawn later in the month. *Alan B. Cross*

Above: In 1945 the Ministry of War Transport permitted London Transport to purchase 20 AEC Regents with Weymann bodies to help alleviate the vehicle shortage problem. They were classified 18STL20 and the entire batch (STL 2682 – 2701) was allocated to Watford High Street Garage in 1946 for use on route 321 and later 351 when the route was split. STL 2691 is seen at Watford Junction in the original green and white livery on route 321. *Alan B. Cross*

In April 1950 a batch of Weymann bodied RTs was allocated to routes 409 and 411 and they were the first to appear in all over green livery. RT 3120 working to West Croydon on route 411 awaits a new crew opposite Godstone Garage. *Alan B. Cross*

A further batch of Weymann bodied vehicles was delivered in Autumn 1950 with some going to Swanley for route 401. In this scene in August 1952 at Eynsford RT 3868 is making the short journey as route 401B back to Swanley Garage where, no doubt, the crew will be finishing their duty, hence the conductor's pleasure. The passengers are waiting for a through 401 towards Dartford. Note the deep style bus stop flag. *Alan B. Cross*

Below left: The British Transport Commission directed that new vehicles for the Tilling Group companies should be temporarily allocated to London Transport to help alleviate the shortage of buses. Most buses went to the Central Area but ten Hants & Dorset Bristol K6A type lowbridge buses went to the Country Area in December 1948 and February 1949 where they were allocated to Amersham, Godstone and Reigate garages. All left London Transport in March 1950. A rear view is seen of Hants & Dorset fleet number TD878 operating on route 410 at Keston. *Bromley Camera Club*

Far right: One further bus to be allocated to the Country Area was this Bristol K5G type from United Automobile Services Ltd, fleet number BDO 109. Having been allocated to Cricklewood Garage in June 1949 it was transferred to Reigate in March 1950 and remained there until the end of May. It is seen heading for Bromley on route 410. All of these borrowed buses had a metal London Transport bullseye sign fixed to the radiator. *Alan B. Cross*

the upper deck with the seats arranged in rows of four. Designated RLH 1–20 they were finished in a pleasing livery of all over Lincoln green with a cream centre band. They were delivered in May and June 1950 with six going to both Amersham and Godstone and eight to Addlestone. The wartime STL19s at Addlestone were sent to Godstone and Reigate to enable the 1934 'Godstone' STLs to be temporarily placed in store. Due to their good condition they went into service again in September 1950 at Addlestone and Guildford garages following changes to the routes in the areas.

An order was placed by London Transport for a further 56 RLHs to be delivered to both the Country and Central areas in 1952 which meant for the first time there would be an adequate number of buses in the lowbridge fleet. A readily distinguishable feature was that they had polished aluminium radiators. Thirty-two buses in green livery (RLH 21–52) went into service in the Country area in October and November 1952 and twenty-one replaced the STL19s and "Godstone" STLs at Addlestone, Godstone and Guildford garages. The balance of eleven was allocated to Amersham for routes 305/A and 359, East Grinstead for 424 and 428 and Guildford for route 415 – none of which required the use of low-height vehicles.

With the replacement of the Green Line Daimlers at Romford by RTs from July 1950 it had been proposed that they be cascaded to Country bus work. Plans were prepared for them to go to Leavesden Road for route 377 and British Railways private hire work, to Watford High Street for 332 and 344 and BR private hire work, to Northfleet for routes 495 and 496 and to Dunton Green for route 431. In the event all of the vehicles concerned were transferred to Central Buses.

Work also commenced on the replacement of the lowbridge fleet in 1950. No doubt London Transport would have preferred to develop its own design but 20 buses were offered by the British Transport Commission which had been ordered but were surplus to Midland General's requirements. They consisted of AEC Regent Mark III chassis with a 9.6 litre engine, pre-selective gears and Weymann bodies. In principle they were mechanically not unlike the RT but in practice had few common units. The 53-seat bodies had a sunken gangway on the offside of

By 1950 London Transport's lowbridge fleet was in urgent need of replacement. ST 1090, seen at the Chesham Nashleigh Arms terminus on route 336, was one of two vehicles dating from 1930 acquired from Amersham & District. *F.G. Reynolds*

ST 140 was one of six randomly numbered low-height buses dating from 1930 acquired from National. The bus is parked on Addlestone Garage forecourt awaiting its next duty on route 462 where it will pass under a low railway bridge between Chertsey and Staines. *F.G. Reynolds*

A batch of 20 buses surplus to Midland General's requirements were offered to London Transport by the British Transport Commission. They had AEC Regent Mark III chassis and Weymann bodywork, became RLH 1–20 in the LT fleet and were delivered between May and July 1950. RLH 20 is seen at Bromley Common heading for Bromley North on route 410. *F.G. Reynolds*

The RLH's interior view shows little concession to the usual LT standards. The sunken upper deck can be seen above the off-side seats and passengers leaving these seats had a good chance of hitting their heads while doing so. The RT seat moquette is one of the few redeeming features. *London Transport Museum*

The upper deck looking towards the stairs shows the sunken gangway and the seats for four passengers. It was a difficult task for the conductor to reach across to collect a fare from the passenger in the window seat when the bus was full. Most passengers would have been at eye level with the top of the sliding windows. *London Transport Museum*

The 'Godstone' STLs were placed into service again in September 1950 at Addlestone and Guildford garages. STL 1050 is seen on Addlestone Garage forecourt. It was finally placed out of stock in January 1953. *LCC Tramways Trust/F.G. Reynolds*

A further batch of 32 RLHs went into service in October and November 1952 which allowed all earlier low-height types to be withdrawn. RLH 40 is seen at Reigate Market Place. *Martin Brown*

Deliveries of RTs in 1951 saw RT 4031–4050 allocated principally to Luton for 321 and Dartford for 467/491. RT 4099–4126 appeared in April and May with the majority being allocated around the garages for Green Line relief duties in the Festival of Britain year. Others went to Dartford to complete the 467/491 and Windsor for the 446 group. The last batch to be allocated to the Country Area in 1951, RT 4161–4207, appeared from June to August and was used to convert 321 and 351 at Watford High Street, 460 at Staines and 495 at Northfleet. As a result some of the 18STL20s were cascaded from Watford High Street to Grays.

The year 1952 saw RT deliveries continue with three batches. RT 3417–3463 arrived in January and February being allocated in the main to Northfleet for 496, Swanley for 477, High Wycombe for 362, 366 and 455A and St Albans for 338, 358. They were followed from April to June by RT 3495–3533 which went to Hertford for 331, 350/A and 395/A, Dorking and Reigate for 429/439, St Albans for 369, East Grinstead for 428; and a start was made on the 423 allocation at Swanley. The final batch, RT 3597–3636, saw the completion of the 423, then Grays for 323A/B, Dunton Green for 431/A and 454, St Albans for 325, 343 and 354, Staines for 441D, 466 and 469, Luton for 356/376, Addlestone for 420, Northfleet for 497/498, Windsor for 457C/D and Hitchin for 392/A. In addition one bus went to Amersham for the 359 and one to Crawley for the Horsham – Roffey Corner shorts on 434.

The year 1953 was momentous for fleet renewals for the Country Area as not only did new RTs continue to come on stream but a start was made on the renewal of both the large saloon and small saloon single-deck fleet. A batch of 37 RTs (RT 3647–3683) arrived between January and March. They went to 13 different garages principally to allow older vehicles to be released for overhaul but they also displaced STLs from routes 407, 442, 453 and 478 and augmented services at Watford High Street and Grays.

Considerable reduction in the number of STLs required for service had been achieved. The allocation book for the commencement of the summer programme on 6th May 1953 reveals that just 54 STLs at 10 garages were required for service as shown opposite.

Top: London Transport had been somewhat embarrassed during and after the war by a shortage of low height buses in both the Central and Country areas and had taken steps to ensure that a similar situation would not occur again. Eleven of the 32 Country Area RLHs were allocated to routes that did not require to be operated by the type. RLH 43 is seen at Dormansland working on route 428 to East Grinstead.

Centre: RT 4046, new in February 1951, was part of batch which was sent to Dartford for routes 467 and 491. The bus is seen on the Sidcup Station stand bound for Wilmington on route 467. Most journeys arriving at Wilmington as 467 would then work to Belvedere on route 491. *F.G. Reynolds*

Left: RT 3418 was new to Northfleet in January 1952 and is seen leaving Rosherville with a well patronised lunch time works journey to Kings Farm Estate on route 488A. *Alan B. Cross*

Garage	M-F	Sat	Sun	Routes
Addlestone	6	1	-	Supplementary schedule
Crawley	1	1	1	483
	6	5	-	Supplementary schedule
Dartford	7	-	-	Supplementary schedule
Dunton Green	2	-	-	Supplementary schedule
Garston	1	1	-	301A
	6	3	-	344 group
	2	-	-	BR private hire
Grays	11	4	-	323, 380 and works services
Hertford	4	4	2	327
	1	1	-	331
	1	1	-	350/A
Hitchin	1	-	-	Private hire contract
Reigate	2	-	-	Chiswick staff bus (1)
Watford High St	-	-	2	311 (hospital journeys)
	3	-	-	BR private hire
Total	54	21	5	

Note: (1) Reigate's staff buses were occasionally used on local routes on a Saturday.

Top: Watford High Street's RT 3682 was one of a batch of 37 buses allocated to 13 garages between January and March 1953 principally to displace STLs and to allow earlier RTs to be released for overhaul. The immaculate bus is seen at New Barnet Station with blinds correctly set. The appearance of RTs was enhanced when without advertisements but advertising was, of course, a valuable source of revenue to London Transport. *Geoff Rixon*

Above: The number of STLs required for service dwindled as new RTs became available and when the summer schedules were introduced in May 1954 only 54 were needed on Monday to Friday being mostly relegated to works services. Roofbox STL 1788 dating from 1937 is seen working a special journey on route 402 from Sevenoaks to Fort Halstead. *LCC Tramways Trust/D. Battams*

A batch of 17 RTs (RT 3719–3735) had been provided for Green Line duplication over the coronation period in June 1953. When no longer required in this role some buses went to Garston for the 344 group releasing seven 18STL20s which went to Hertford for route 327 where a weak bridge over the New River precluded the use of post-war RTs. In October a further batch of green RTs (RT 3807–3816) not immediately required for use as Country buses were allocated to Southall Garage in the Central Area.

A total of 59 green STLs were relicensed for the month of June and allocated across the network in order to cover for RTs which were needed for heavy Green Line duplication and tours over the coronation route. They included 23 front entrance type with both Chiswick and Weymann bodies which had not seen service since 1951. Even more surprisingly seven low-height buses (three STL19s and four Godstones) were also relicensed with one bus, STL 1051, allocated to Garston! At some garages they did little or no work and all were withdrawn on 1st July thus ending service of the front entrance and low-height STLs in the Country Area.

More RT deliveries spanning from May 1954 until December 1955 comprised RT 4510–4556 plus seven in the 47xx series enabled the displacement of all of the remaining pre-war STLs. Addlestone's went on 1st August 1954, followed by those at Crawley and Dartford on 11th August. The remaining 24 left in service, of which 15 were in red livery, at Dunton Green, Garston, Grays, Hertford and Hitchin ran in service for the last time on 31st August. The withdrawal of the post-war 18STL20s at Garston and Grays came on 1st May 1955. The Hertford buses continued in service for another month to be replaced on 1st June by seven RT2s (RT 36, 62, 79, 93, 114, 128 and 137) of 1940/41 vintage which were painted into green livery. These vehicles weighed 15cwt less than the standard RT and could thus operate on route 327. In practice seven vehicles were generous for route 327 and they made frequent appearances on other routes including Green Line 715 relief workings. The troublesome bridge was rebuilt in August 1957 and on 1st September the seven green RT2s were demoted to staff buses or used for driver training when post-war RTs took over on the route.

By the beginning of 1955 approximately 917 green RTs had been delivered including 57 vehicles in Green Line livery which were allocated to Grays and Romford London Road garages. London Transport now found itself with an embarrassing surplus of double-deck vehicles with a number of new RTs placed into store. Predictions of future vehicle requirements had proved optimistic and passenger usage was now in decline which affected service levels. This decline in passenger numbers was more acute in the Central Area as in the Country Area the growth of the new towns and new housing development in general had offset declines in more traditional areas. The RT2s had been withdrawn from passenger service in the Central Area, which allowed seven to be transferred to the Country Area. The non-standard Craven RTs had all been withdrawn from the Central Area by May 1956 and, incredibly, 23 of them had been repainted green and despatched to Watford High Street and Windsor. They were destined not to remain at their new homes for long as the last green Cravens were withdrawn from Windsor on 17th October 1956. New RTs in the 47xx series were released from store for use in the Country Area in May 1956, March and April 1958 and from March 1959 with the last, RT 4773, going to Northfleet in August 1959 after being used in passenger loading experiments.

RT 4794 was in store for 18 months before being allocated to East Grinstead in November 1955. The bus on route 424 has worked a short journey to Woodhatch, The Beehive and is seen on the stand in Sandcross Lane. Note the temporary bus stop sign. *Alan B. Cross/Roy Hobbs*

London Transport's Country Buses & Coaches operating department also had a flourishing tours and excursions business. For the summer season in 1951 some 105 tours were offered across the network to places of interest such as Chessington Zoo, Hampton Court, London Airport, Tunbridge Wells, Whipsnade Zoo and Windsor. Sporting events including Ascot and Epsom races, Brands Hatch and Wimbledon Speedway were catered for as well as scenic and River Thames tours. The most expensive outing was from Hertford to Ascot and Epsom on special race days when a premium fare of 10 shillings was charged. A rather more modest Sunday evening tour from Gravesend to the Darenth Valley could be had for 2 shillings and 6 pence. In the winter season 24 different football excursions were offered from across the network to Charlton, Chelsea, Fulham, Highbury (Arsenal) and Tottenham. Seven different excursions were offered to bonfire celebrations at Edenbridge and Lingfield in November and in the post-Christmas season 40 excursions were offered to circuses and ice shows which included combined fares and admission prices. London Transport's private hire operation was constrained by distance and was unable to operate further afield, for example to the coast.

Green Line 10T10, T 504, lays over at an unknown location having worked an excursion from Hertford. *Alan B. Cross*

The year 1951 was Festival of Britain year and London Transport had decided to acquire 40 coaches of two distinct types for private hire, tours and excursions work. One batch numbered RF 1–25 were 35 seaters all allocated to Central Buses delivery of which commenced in May – the RF will be described below. Delivered simultaneously RFW 1–15 were ECW bodied coaches mounted on the AEC Regal IV 9821E chassis. They were built to new maximum permitted dimensions for single-deck vehicles of 30 feet long and 8 feet wide. While the RFs were buses with coach trimmings the RFWs had been designed as coaches proper. They seated 39

passengers in high-back seats with headrests and the driving cab was not partitioned. Six coaches were initially allocated to Country Buses as follows: RFW 3 Reigate, RFW 5 Watford, Leavesden Road, RFW 6 Romford, London Road, RFW 10 Northfleet, RFW 12 Windsor and RFW 14 also to Romford. Mr Harbour, the Operating Manager, directed that the RFWs were to be used on private hire work and not, initially, on tours and excursions. He added that under no circumstances were they to be used on stage carriage duties or on staff hires. Each garage had a panel of drivers who had been trained on private hire, tour and excursion work.

A posed interior view of an RFW looking forward with a guide giving a commentary by microphone to the passengers. These vehicles were finished to full coach specification including high-back seats. The driver is in summer uniform wearing his white cap cover and lightweight jacket. *London Transport Museum*

In 1951 London Transport acquired 15 RFW purpose built coaches for private hire and tour work. Six were allocated to the Country Area including RFW 5, seen here, which initially went to Watford, Leavesden Road and later Garston. Note the outward opening hinged door. *Alan B. Cross*

As a precursor to ordering the RF class this AEC Regal IV demonstrator with a Park Royal body was extensively trialled entering service at St Albans Garage on route 355 in May 1950. It was subsequently tested on route 447 at Reigate. Originally produced as a 40 seater the seating capacity had been reduced to 36 by the time it ran in service. *Omnibus Society*

With a view to designing a class of large saloon single deckers which could be adapted for use across all London Transport, a demonstrator, UMP 227, entered service at St Albans Garage on route 355 in May 1950. The AEC chassis was classified "Regal IV" and it was fitted with a Park Royal body in 1949. It was built to the then maximum permitted length of 27ft. 6ins. and the chassis was fitted with the AEC 9.6 litre RT engine modified to operate in a horizontal position. The transmission was similar to that of the RT and when new the body was fitted with 40 seats. By the time the bus entered service with London Transport the seating capacity had been reduced to 36. London Transport's engineers were obviously satisfied and an order was made for 700 chassis units. The bodies were, however, ordered from Metro-Cammell rather than Park Royal. The first batch was 25 private hire coaches, each seating 35 passengers, which were delivered in May and June 1951. Ministry of Transport regulations had been amended to permit a maximum length of 30 feet for single-deck vehicles and the remainder of the class were extended to this length. RF 26–288 were built as Green Line coaches being delivered between October 1951 and November 1952 and RF 289–513 were Central Buses delivered between September 1952 and March 1953. The Country Area buses, RF 514–699, were delivered between March and December 1953 with RF 517, 647 and 700 being modified for one-man operation before entering service in March 1954. The Country Bus version of the RF seated 41 passengers and differed from the Central Area version by being fitted with air operated doors which the Metropolitan police would still not permit on Central Area buses. They were classified 2RF2/2.

RF 514, the first of the batch of 187 Country buses, is posed for the London Transport official photographer. The pleasing lines of what was to become the standard London Transport single-deck bus are readily apparent. The jack-knife doors have been captured either opening or closing. This bus was allocated to Reigate initially for route 447. *London Transport Museum*

RF 647 was one of three buses modified for one-man operation which did not enter service until March 1954. Note the discreet 'Pay as you enter' transfer in gold lettering at the top of the nearside windscreen. Following an accident to a member of staff a black horizontal bar was fitted across the nearside windscreen on all RF type vehicles. The one-man buses were initially trialled on route 419. *London Transport Museum*

These two views show the modifications applied to RF 647 for one-man operation. The wider cab has an opening window fitted behind the driver and the used ticket box has been repositioned from the driver's door. The nearside long seat has been reduced in length to seat three persons and a small luggage pen fitted. A mirror has been fitted to the front bulkhead to enable the driver to see the passenger saloon. A glass screen has been fitted to the driver's door together with a cash desk and the two Ultimate ticket machines are shown in position. *Alan B Cross*

The delivery of the Green Line RFs had permitted the displaced 10T10s and TFs in turn to displace some 4Q4s, 6Q6s and older T types from Country Bus duties. There was a proposal to modify the TFs allocated to bus work by repositioning the nearside front seat longitudinally to allow more space for the conductor to stand and move the faretable holder from the rear emergency door to the front bulkhead, but in view of the limited time for which they would be used as buses, the cost could not be justified. The first RF batch (RF 514–516, 518–531, 552, 557, 613) perhaps unsurprisingly, went to Reigate initially for route 447 and were quickly followed by the balance for routes 406C and 440/A where they usurped the last stronghold of the 4Q4 type. A report noted that there was some degree of late running on the 447 during the first week of operation but once drivers were fully familiar with the type the situation improved considerably. The management and staff were pleased with them although some concern was expressed about the narrow entrance and the effect on boarding and alighting times.

Top: Former 10T10 Green Line coach T 604 was new in 1938 and is seen leaving Luton for Flamstead on route 356. *Alan B. Cross*

Above left: Towards the end of their lives some 10T10s were painted into red livery for use in the Central Area. T 580 was initially despatched to Addlestone after repaint on 10th October 1951 but five days later was transferred to Kingston. It is seen standing on the forecourt at Addlestone Garage. It still retains the brackets for the Green Line side route boards. *LCC Tramways Trust/F.G. Reynolds*

Above right: The 4Q4 type, originally consisting of 102 vehicles dating from 1935/6, was one of the main classes of single decker before the arrival of the RF. Q 50 is seen working one of the 402 special journeys from Fort Halstead to Sevenoaks in September 1951. *Alan B. Cross/Allen T. Smith*

Left: T 364 was acquired from Amersham & District in 1933 and was rebodied in 1938 and designated 11T11. The bus is seen at the Totteridge terminus of the short route 363 from High Wycombe in January 1950. *John Gillham/Tony Peters*

Q231 is one of a batch of 50 Green Line coaches designated 6Q6 and delivered in 1936/7. As they were displaced from Green Line work by the introduction of RFs, they were cascaded to bus duties to replace some of the older large saloons. Working on route 391, the bus awaits a new crew opposite St Albans Garage while heading for Hill End.
Alan B. Cross

TF 25 is one of a batch of 75 Green Line coaches built in 1939 to a revolutionary design: the first true under-floor engine single-decker. Displaced from Green Line duties, the vehicle has been repainted in all over green bus livery with the London Transport fleetname. It is seen outside St Albans Garage in June 1952.
Alan B. Cross

The first RF Country Buses went to Reigate in March 1953 for use on route 447. RF 530 is seen with a good load of passengers on this busy service. The destination blind layout was a standard style for circuitous or indirect services.
F.G. Reynolds

The new buses were subsequently allocated as follows: to St Albans for routes 365/391, 355, 304 and 382, Hertford (372, 342, 308/384/399 and 390), Luton (364, 356/376), Hitchin (308/384/399, 364, 390), Windsor (458, 407A), Dorking (425), Guildford (432, 425), Garston (318/A), High Wycombe (363), Leatherhead (422, 435, 462, 419), Addlestone (462, 427/437/456), Two Waters (322, 337), Dunton Green (404, 421), East Grinstead (424, 434/473), Crawley (434/473), Epping (308/384/399) and Northfleet (489/A). Displaced 15T13s from Garston and Two Waters went to Crawley for, initially, 434/473, Tring for 352 and 387, Hatfield for duplication and Grays for 375, thus displacing the last TFs from bus work. Some RF buses also initially served as Green Line spares. Following the introduction of route 725 on 1st July 1953, there were insufficient Green Line RF spares until the conversion of the 723 group from RF to RT on 7th July 1954. By mid-1954 the following routes were worked by the 15T13s of 1948 vintage: Two Waters (307, 317/A), Grays (375), Tring (352, 387), Amersham (394 group) and Crawley (426 and works). The conversion of routes 318/A to RT operation on 19th May 1954 had allowed the displaced 15T13s to go to Amersham. The few remaining 10T10s were displaced as a knock-on effect of double-decking of Green Line 723/A. Released RF coaches replaced Country bus RFs being used as Green Line spares around the fleet. Routes 412 (Dorking), 413/A (Dunton Green), a works/ contract bus at Hitchin and a miscellaneous supplementary working on 441/466/469 at Staines were converted to RFs with the last day of 10T10 operation being 6th July 1954.

Brand new RF 533 approaches Allum Lane Corner at Elstree and is seen on route 355 heading for St Albans, Lancaster Road. The absence of other road traffic was a typical feature of the period. *Dilwyn Rees*

Addlestone's RF 640 is seen working on route 456 heading for Woking at West Byfleet. *London Transport Museum*

The old and new stand side-by-side at Rickmansworth Station Car Park. C 60 was outstationed at Loudwater Estate for route 336A. Garston received an allocation of RFs for the 318 group but RF 618 has been used to substitute for a 15T13 on route 309. *LCC Tramway Trust/D. Battams*

After the introduction of the RF buses routes 307 and 317/A at Two Waters remained worked by the 15T13 class dating from 1948. The complexities of interworking show T 777 working to Apsley Mills on route 377A which was a route normally worked by double deckers. *Alan B. Cross*

T 685 was painted into all over green bus livery and allocated to Dunton Green until its withdrawal on 1st January 1954. The bus awaits passengers for Shoreham Village on route 404 at Sevenoaks Bus Station.

London Transport conducted comparison trials between the RFs and three lightweight single deckers, all in Green Line livery, commencing in 1953. One vehicle was this Bristol LS5G with a body by Eastern Coach Works, registration number PHW918, which was loaned by Bristol Tramways and Carriage Company Ltd. The bus entered service on route 447 in April 1953. *D.W.K. Jones*

The RF was a very heavy vehicle and by the time the Country Area examples were being delivered, vehicle builders were developing lightweight single deckers. London Transport decided to conduct some comparative trials between the RF and three light-weight single deckers. A Bristol LS5G with an Eastern Coach Works 6110 Series 2 body was loaned by Bristol Tramways and Carriage Company Ltd. Registered PHW 918, the 45-seater was turned out in Green Line livery and initially had an unladen weight of 6 tons 7cwt 2qtr. It went to Reigate for use on route 447 on 23rd April 1953 and was subsequently used on Green Line route 711 before being returned to Bristol where it was fitted with Hobbs semi-automatic transmission. It returned to Reigate on 26th August 1953 for use on route 447 until November, albeit with a return to Bristol Tramways in the September. On 6th November 1953 it was transferred to Dalston for use on Central Area routes 208/A. After a return to Chiswick and the manufacturer it appeared on route 447 again on 5th March 1954 now fitted with a Gardner 6-cylinder diesel engine until return to Chiswick on 21st April 1954. The bus was subsequently returned to Bristol Tramways and saw no further service with LT.

The second vehicle (PTE 592) was a Leyland Tiger Cub PSUC1/1 fitted with a 44-seat body by Saunders Roe. Finished in Green Line livery, it had a centrifugal clutch, an RV16 semi-automatic gear box and Eaton two-speed rear axle. It had an unladen weight of 5 tons 12cwt. Allocated to Reigate on 25th June 1953 it appeared on route 447 and subsequently route 711. It went to Dalston on 12th November but was back at Reigate on 1st December for route 447, returned to Dalston on 19th March 1954, and eventually returned to Chiswick and Leyland Motors Ltd.

The remaining vehicle was an AEC Monocoach demonstrator with a 44-seat Park Royal body registered NLP 635 and turned out initially in Green Line livery. It was fitted with an AH410 6.75 litre engine with a pre-selective gearbox similar to an RT's. It weighed one hundredweight less than the Tiger Cub. It went to Reigate on 28th August 1953 for use on 447 and later 711, then to Dalston on 18th January 1954. It was returned to AEC on 30th April 1954 but was loaned again for route 447 from January 1956 until May 1957, this time fitted with "Monocontrol" transmission which was developed by AEC to replace the pre-selective gearbox. London Transport did not order any new types of single-deck buses as a result of these trials. It was curious that the trials should be conducted when LT was taking delivery of the last of 700 RFs for which the accountants allocated a book life of 14 years. Most of them were to remain in service for considerably longer.

The second vehicle was a
Leyland Tiger Cub PSUC1/I
fitted with a Saunders Roe
body. *F.G. Reynolds*

The third bus was an AEC
Monocoach with a Park Royal
body which entered service at
Reigate in August 1953.
The bus is seen in Redhill.
F.G. Reynolds

There were concerns at the ever increasing costs of operation particularly on some of the more rural routes where passenger numbers were starting to decline. Single manning was an obvious economy and the idea of flat fare operation had been tried outside London but was not considered acceptable for operation on rural routes. A delegation from London Transport visited the Huddersfield Joint Omnibus Committee in 1952 where an experiment running 43-seater single-deck Guy Arabs using one-man operation was being tried. The LT delegation was impressed and three buses (RF 517, 647 and 700) were set aside for conversion. They were fitted with wider cabs to accommodate a change-giving machine and provision to house two Ultimate type ticket machines. The driver's door was extended to the top of the opening, projected to the front bulkhead and fitted with two glass screens, the main one having openings not unlike those found in a cinema cashier's office at the time. A cab light for night time operation was installed. The drivers were provided with two Ultimate ticket issuing machines. A sliding opening window was fitted behind the driver and a reversing light provided at the rear. To aid passenger access on account of the wider cab the two leading nearside longitudinal seats were replaced by a small luggage pen. The buses were equipped with 'Pay as you enter' signs. They were allocated to Leatherhead for use from 3rd March 1954 on route 419 (Langley Vale – Epsom, Brettgrave). On 11th August route 419 reverted to crew operation; the OMO equipped buses were transferred to Two Waters for route 316 (Chesham – Adeyfield). The experiment was regarded as a success and a programme for converting many rural routes to OMO was drawn up. The cost of converting the buses had been quite expensive and the majority of the class would be more simply equipped, dispensing with the wide cab, driver's screen and change-giving machine. The drivers would now be provided with only one Ultimate machine.

The driver of RF 169 seems to have manoeuvred himself into a situation where he is unable to move his charge in either direction while working on route 447 in Redhill. *Alan B. Cross/Allen T. Smith*

A complicated renumbering process of the RF class took place between January and May 1956 when some 35 vehicles from the Private Hire, Central Bus and Country Bus fleets were converted to Green Line coaches. The Country Area vehicles affected were as follows:

RF 514–16 Converted for Green Line operation and renumbered RF 295–7

RF 517 One-man equipped bus renumbered RF 697

RF 518–32 Converted for Green Line operation and renumbered RF 299–313

RF 647/49 One-man equipped buses renumbered RF 698/9

RF 697 Converted for Green Line operation and renumbered RF 298

RF 698/9 Renumbered RF 647/49

These changes resulted in a loss of 19 RF buses from the Country fleet. Following these changes RF 682–696 were then withdrawn from service for conversion to one-man operated

vehicles taking up their new duties in July. For subsequent conversions vehicles were taken at random.

After the one-man conversions in May 1959 some redeployment of the fleet was undertaken in order to release subsequent RF buses for conversion. A number of Green Line RFs required for Monday to Friday relief duties were replaced by surplus RTs and, in turn, drafted on to the busier routes that were to remain crew operated. These were the 391 group at St Albans, 447 group at Reigate and 458 at Windsor. The vehicles concerned were not altered in any way and retained their Green Line livery. The Country bus RFs released from these routes were then converted for one-man operation taking up their duties on 10th June 1959. There were no doubt some double-deck routes that were suitable for conversion to single-deck one-man operation but a lack of vehicles meant that there would be no further such conversions until November 1964.

RF 16–25 were originally private hire fleet coaches that were modified for Green Line work in 1956. In this view of RF 16 working on route 447 the right hand indicator is actually on being capable of flashing at a rate of 76 times per minute. Note the different arrangement of the roof board bracket fittings due to the position of the roof windows. *Alan B. Cross/Allen T. Smith*

The summer schedules for 1953 required 58 small saloon, one-man operated buses plus traffic spares. The majority of the fleet consisted of Leyland Cubs dating from 1935 and their replacement had become a matter of some urgency. C 34 is seen in rural surroundings working on route 433 from Dorking Garage. Note the blind display 'Coldharbour for Leith Hill'. When East Surrey pioneered the route the intention had been to run to Leith Hill but the state of the roads meant that the route could not run beyond Coldharbour.
Alan B. Cross

The need to replace the small saloon fleet consisting mostly of C class Leyland Cubs dating from 1935, supplemented by a few of the ill-fated CR class of 1939, was pressing. The need for small saloons had decreased considerably during the war due to an increase in passenger demand and at the end of the hostilities, only 32 were required for service. From 1948 London Transport had introduced a number of rural routes in areas not previously served and by May 1953 some 58 small saloons were needed. Due to the small number required the expense of a pure London Transport design could not be justified and in 1952, an order was placed with Guy Motors Ltd. for 84 chassis based on the Otter and Vixen models and fitted with Perkins 4.73 litre diesel engines and crash gearboxes (designated GS 1–84). The 26-seat bodies were ordered from Eastern Coach Works and the end result was an unmistakably provincial vehicle with some London Transport refinements. The first example had been expected to be available in August of that year but Guy Motors had encountered difficulties due to their unfamiliarity with London Transport's design requirements primarily as regards accessibility for maintenance. The delay in chassis production disrupted ECW's production schedule which exacerbated the delay and the first vehicle was delivered one year later than envisaged. In the meantime the Cs and CRs were obliged to soldier on.

It was originally proposed to order approximately 70 buses but there was felt to be scope to convert some of the less busy large saloon routes to GS operation so the order was increased to 84. In anticipation of new regulations they were the first LT buses to be fitted from new with two rear red reflectors. GS 2 went into service in October 1953 at Hitchin on route 383 and the Cs and CRs were quickly replaced with the last CR being withdrawn from Swanley in November and the last C from Tring in January 1954. In addition the Guys usurped large saloons as follows: Northfleet route 492 in December, Hertford routes 329/A, 386/A (Saturday excepted) and 389 on 21st April 1954, Garston routes 309, 361 on 19th May and Windsor routes 442, 445 on 14th July.

C 23 is seen at Hertford Bus Station having worked a journey on route 388. The bus has been painted into the all over green bus livery. The enquiry office and waiting room is seen in the background. *Alan B. Cross*

The replacement for the Cubs was obtained from Guy Motors Ltd. fitted with a Perkins diesel engine and 26-seat body by Eastern Coach Works. Dubbed 'Guy Special' they were numbered GS 1–84. Newly delivered GS 1 has been posed for inspection by management and officials. As was a common occurrence with official photographs any convenient blind to hand was fitted. The type did not work on route 424. *ECW Archives S.J. Butler collection*

GS 2 is shown to a group of drivers by an instructor at Chiswick Works. Note the Guy emblem of the head of a Red Indian chief and the slogan 'Feathers in our cap' on the bonnet. While possessing some London Transport attributes the buses were very much of a provincial nature. *London Transport Museum*

In 1949 the London Transport Executive had taken the decision that the trolleybus fleet should be replaced by motor buses at the end of its useful life. To this end a new design of motor bus was developed – the Routemaster. There were four prototypes with the first vehicle, RM 1, being exhibited at the Commercial Motor Show in September 1954. The bus was very extensively tested and modified before it entered revenue-earning service in February 1956. A second vehicle, broadly the same as RM 1, was taken into stock in March 1955 and it too underwent very extensive tests and modifications. The passenger saloons had a number of differences from those in RM 1. RM 2 was originally fitted with a smaller capacity AEC AV470 engine which was rated at 7.68 litres and London Transport seemed in no rush for the bus to enter service. It was subsequently fitted with a 9.6 litre engine, which necessitated alterations to the front end, and painted into Country Bus livery, entering service (with considerably less publicity than was afforded to RM 1) at Reigate Garage on routes 406 and 406A on 20th May 1957. It seemingly encountered a number of mechanical problems while on trial and its use was rather irregular. The bus returned to Chiswick on 8th August 1957 and was subsequently repainted into red livery for use at Turnham Green Garage. Country Buses' higher management was somewhat lukewarm at the trial of what was intended to be developed as a high specification vehicle primarily to operate in an urban environment as a trolleybus replacement being tested on one of its routes. Mr Fernyhough, the Operating Manager, who was very well connected within the bus industry, had noted that some of provincial operators, notably Southdown, used double-deck buses with doors and he tended to favour the arrangement. At this stage the bulk of the double-deck fleet consisted of open platform RTs so it was a case of biding his time. It was destined to be eight years before a batch of Routemaster buses was allocated to the Country Area.

Top and centre: Somewhat remarkably route 442 running from Slough to Farnham Royal lost its RTs in favour of the new GS type on 14th July 1954. These two views at Slough Station show RT 3446 and GS 76 working on the route. *Ron Wellings*

Left: In this rural scene at Betsham, GS meets GS! GS 47 is running from Dartford to Kingsdown on route 452 and an unidentified member of the class is proceeding from Gravesend to Dartford on route 450. Both buses seem to be suffering from a severe lack of patronage. Note the small style bus stop flag. *M.G. Webber Collection*

Some 15 additional GSs had been incorporated into the order to allow some crew-operated routes to be converted to one-man operation. One such route was the 361 from Rickmansworth to Chorleywood which lost its 15T13s in favour of the GS. GS 76 stands at Rickmansworth Station Car Park.

Routemaster prototype RM 2 was turned out in green livery and sent to Reigate Garage in May 1957 for use on routes 406/A. The bus encountered mechanical problems during its spell at Reigate and was returned to Chiswick in August. The Country Area management were reputedly less than enthusiastic about the trial. It is seen here in an official posed London Transport view and in service at Tadworth Station on route 406A. Note that the word 'route' was applied above the offside route number box. *London Transport Museum, Alan B.Cross*

CHAPTER 3 — ACQUISITIONS

On 7th June 1950 London Transport took over the service between Loudwater Estate and Rickmansworth Met. Station from Land & Estates Ltd. The service which dated from 1928 was primarily provided as a train feeder and shoppers' facility from the exclusive private estate. The service was numbered 336A and the bus was outstationed on the estate returning once a week to Leavesden Road Garage for servicing or substitution. In this posed view passengers board C 60 by a thatched cottage on the estate. *London Transport Museum*

The acquisition of services from other operators was by no means confined to the early years of London Transport. On 7th June 1950 London Transport acquired the Loudwater Bus Service from Land & Estates Ltd which ran a route from the exclusive Loudwater Estate to Rickmansworth Met. Station. The service had run since March 1928 but had been suspended during the Second World War. At one time a second route had been provided between Rickmansworth and Capel Hamlet, near Chorleywood Station but this service was not resumed after the war. London Transport had allowed this service, which ran entirely within the Special area, to continue as it was regarded as being uneconomic. Following the death of the proprietor, Cameron Jeffs, his executors offered the service to London Transport which, as no other operator was prepared to take it over, reluctantly agreed to continue operating it. Some of the uneconomic Country Area routes were financed by cross-subsidisation where they were supported by the profitable routes. The service ran Monday to Saturday peak hours with odd trips for shoppers in between. The route was allocated the number 336A and worked by a C from Leavesden Road garage which was outstationed on the estate in the old coach house. The existing driver was employed by the Executive and paid in his takings at Rickmansworth station booking office. The bus went to Leavesden Road Garage on Saturdays for servicing.

A long standing independent operator, Sargents of East Grinstead Ltd, sold out to Southdown Motor Services on 25th March 1951. It operated three routes from East Grinstead to Ashurst Wood, Crowborough and Edenbridge which were all subsequently passed to Maidstone & District. On 24th February 1948 a works service to Crawley had been introduced which Southdown initially operated without a route number. From 30th April 1951 the service was passed to London Transport and received the route numbers 438 and 438A. Under London Transport auspices, taking into account the development of Crawley New Town, the arrangements were destined to become increasingly complicated. Initially both routes consisted of just one journey in each direction on Monday to Friday. Route 438 ran from East Grinstead Bus Station to Crawley Garage via Felbridge over the direct route 424 to Copthorne and then via Shipley Bridge, Tinsley Green, Gatwick Airport and Lowfield Heath. The 438A ran direct from Tinsley Green avoiding Lowfield Heath. It should

be noted that Gatwick Airport was a considerably smaller establishment than it is today – the timing point was 'Gatwick Airport *Control Tower*'! There was a subsequent item in the Traffic Circular for a terminal working there where drivers were instructed not to cross the white line marking the runway. The routes were worked by 4Q4s from Crawley Garage and positioning journeys between Crawley Garage and East Grinstead Bus Station were run in both directions via route 434 from Crawley to Copthorne thence as route 424 to East Grinstead both direct and via Crawley Down. Incredibly these journeys ran under the number 424, which now consisted of a main route between Reigate and East Grinstead (Stone Quarry Estate) with two intermediate bifurcations via Duxhurst or Irons Bottom and Snow Hill or Crawley Down, shuttles from Horley to Horne and Horley to Outwood Common and positioning journeys from Crawley to East Grinstead. In other instances even the most minor variation to a route was deemed to warrant a suffix letter.

STL 1641 is seen working from Windsor to Slough Trading Estate on route 407 which had been established by Mr J.A. Perry and passed to London Transport on 1st July 1951. At this period new RTs were to be found on the trunk services and STLs remained the preserve of works services. The bus follows three RTs in Windsor Road, Slough and the conductor has positioned himself on the platform ready to give the left hand signal when the bus turns into Slough High Street a few yards ahead. *Alan B. Cross*

An old-established operator based in Windsor, J.A. Perry, had commenced running in 1928 between Windsor and Slough Trading Estate (Dover Road) and while most of the service ran directly between Eton and Slough a handful of journeys ran via Chalvey avoiding Slough town centre. It was these odd journeys that proved to be Perry's salvation as Chalvey was outside the Board's area and London Transport had consented to his continued operation. Mr Perry retired in July 1950 selling out to Crescent Coaches whose proprietor, R.E. Jackson, sought to dispose of the above services together with one from Slough to Cippenham to Thames Valley. Under a joint agreement with London Transport the services to the Trading Estate became routes 407 and 407A via Chalvey and Thames Valley took over the Cippenham route from 1st July 1951. Under the Transport Act, 1947, London Transport was now able to operate via Chalvey. The route was worked from Windsor by one STL on Monday to Saturday plus one T on Monday to Friday providing a peak hour and lunch time service for the Trading Estate workers.

With the withdrawal of the STLs the RTs eventually came to be found on works services. RT 3859 is seen on route 407. *LTPS/D.A. Jones*

The London Passenger Transport Act of 1933 was designed to co-ordinate services across the London area. This had been achieved with the exception of the towns on the boundary of the LPTB area where the operation of cross town services was not permitted. While this may not have been a major problem in other towns, the notable exception was Grays. There was a high level of passenger traffic from Purfleet and West Thurrock to Tilbury which prior to the implementation of the Act in this area had been possible by Eastern National bus or by one of the many small independents. Under the revised arrangements that applied from 18th April 1934 a change at Grays was required to complete such a journey. Not untypically when the bureaucrats get something wrong it takes a generation before it is corrected. Under the auspices of the British Transport Commission an agreement was reached with the London Transport Executive and Eastern National (a Tilling Group company and also part of the BTC) for the former to take over certain services to the east of the old boundary in the Grays area. The first stage of the transfer commenced on 30th September 1951 when 13 routes together with the ownership of Argent Street Depot in Grays were transferred to London Transport. A fleet of 28 buses, some of which were not used in service before being returned to Eastern National, was loaned to LT. The fleet comprised 19 single deckers (six Dennis Lancets, two Bedford OBs, six Bristol JO5Gs and five Bristol L5Gs) and ten Guy Arab II double deckers. The buses had underlined London Transport fleetname stickers applied to the side panels, LTE legal lettering, and as was usual with loaned vehicles, London Transport was never hesitant to puncture the panel work by the fitting of stencil holders. The plan was to close the Argent Street premises operationally from 2nd January 1952 when a major route organisation in the area would absorb the acquired routes into the Country Area network. Argent Street was coded GA but it would have been wasteful to produce stencils for just three months so GY plates were used but, together with the running number plates, they were painted red which denoted operation from Argent Street. Nine red STLs were allocated to Argent Street on day one and by mid-December there were 23, both red and green. This enabled the early release of some Eastern National buses.

Top: This 31-seater Bristol JO5G numbered 3722 in the Eastern National fleet is fitted with a body built by Eastern Counties and dates from 1937. London Transport fleetname and legal lettering has been applied and the garage stencils have been painted red to denote operation from Argent Street. It is working a short journey to Orsett on route 44. *Alan B. Cross*

Centre: A Bristol L5G, 3898 in the Eastern National fleet, is working on Grays local route 85 and is seen at the Woodside Estate terminus. This bus dates from 1946. *W.J. Haynes*

Right: Utility Guy Arab I 5LW with Brush bodywork, Eastern National 3880 dates from 1943 and is seen on route 31 between Grays and Tilbury, Feenan Highway on 30th September 1951, the first day of London Transport operation. *Alan B. Cross*

Nine STLs had been transferred to Argent Street from day one and others gradually joined them which allowed the Eastern National buses to be released. STL 1784, new to Merton Garage in February 1937, was painted green in November 1951 and transferred to Argent Street. It is seen outside the Queen's Hotel in Grays working on route 31 to Tilbury, Feenan Highway via Dock Road on 29th November 1951. In the rear view, STL 1521, which had been painted green in November 1951, is seen in Grays heading for Shell Haven on works service 35 which was to become 349 after the re-organisation of services.
Alan B. Cross

A surviving independent operator, Benjamin, who traded as 'Our Bus Service', and ran two routes to Nutberry Corner and Fairway jointly with Eastern National, surrendered his share of the licences on 16th September and continued to operate a private hire and excursion business. Routes taken over from Eastern National were:

31   Grays – Tilbury (Feenan Highway)
32   Grays – Orsett (section only)
32A Grays – Nutberry Corner (formerly joint with Our Bus)
32B Grays – Fairway (formerly joint with Our Bus)

35   Grays – Coryton via Shell Haven (works journeys)
37A Grays – Tilbury Ferry via Chadwell St Mary
37B Tilbury Docks – Chadwell St Mary (works journeys)
44   Grays – Bulphan
45   Grays – Linford (section only)
57   Tilbury Docks – Nutberry Corner (works journeys)
81   Tilbury Docks – East Tilbury (Bata Shoe Factory) (special journeys)
82   Grays – East Tilbury (Bata Shoe Factory) (special journeys)
85   Grays – Woodside Estate

Towards the end of December 1951 RTs, but not new ones, were transferred to Argent Street. RT 4038, new to Luton in February 1951, is seen at the alighting point in Orsett Road, Grays near the War Memorial on 1st January 1952, the day before the reorganisation. RT 4119 is seen in Orsett Road, Grays on 1st January 1952 where the conductor is just about to change the front blind for the next working.
Alan B. Cross

The London Transport boundary was extended eastwards to include Orsett, Bulphan and Linford. Stanford-le-Hope was not included although the 35 ran to the east thereof. This meant that route 32 was split at Orsett and route 45 was split at Linford with Eastern National providing shuttles onwards to Stanford-le-Hope. London Transport bus stop flags replaced the Ministry of Transport ones in the new territory.

The three months' period between the take-over and the relocation to Grays London Transport Garage in London Road, where additional outside standing space was provided, allowed the transferred staff to be assimilated into LT ways of working and conditions of service. All drivers and conductors received nine hours of training in three sessions with the drivers receiving instruction on Q, RT and TF vehicles. The conductors must have considered losing their Setright Speed tickets machines for the Bell Punch ticket system a retrograde step. No doubt the transferred staff welcomed London Transport's higher rates of pay. Special five-day weekly tickets were available to the Bata Shoe Factory and Thames Haven and this facility was continued by London Transport, with the tickets being issued by the employers. An Eastern National fares revision on 18th November saw certain fares increased by a halfpenny and this was also applied on the routes taken over. In keeping with past practice Christmas Day services were provided on routes 31, 32B, 35 and 37A. Under the new arrangements Grays required 11 additional RTs and they began to arrive at Argent Street towards the end of the year. They were not brand new vehicles but came mostly from a batch that had been allocated around the garages in May 1951 for Green Line relief duties in connection with the Festival of Britain. The former Eastern National drivers must have found them rather superior compared with the types that they had been used to.

The new network of routes was introduced on 2nd January 1952 when all of the acquired routes were withdrawn and replaced as follows:

323 New route Grays – Orsett – Bulphan replacing routes 32 and 44. One works journey from Orsett to Purfleet Station via West Thurrock.

323A New route Purfleet Station (works journeys) – Grays – Nutberry Corner replacing the 32A.

323B New route Purfleet Station (works journeys) – Grays – Fairway replacing route 32B.

328 New route Ockendon Station – Aveley – Stonehouse Corner – Grays – Woodside Estate and works journeys Ockendon Station – Purfleet Station replacing 85 and 370A.

328A New route Purfleet Station – Stonehouse Corner – Grays – Woodside Estate (works journeys) replacing routes 85 and part 371A.

349 New route Grays – MEC Refineries – Shell Haven – Coryton (works journeys) replacing route 35. MEC Refineries was a bifurcation from the main route with some journeys terminating there and others double running to Shell Haven or Coryton.

357 New route Tilbury Docks – Nutberry Corner (works journeys) replacing route 57.

367 New route Tilbury Docks – Bata Shoe Factory (special journeys) replacing route 81.

368 New route Grays – Bata Shoe Factory via Chadwell Road (special journeys) replacing route 82. Certain duplicate journeys run via Southend Road, Socketts Heath and Woodview instead of Chadwell Road direct.

370 Romford – Grays. Extended from Grays to Tilbury Ferry via Chadwell St Mary replacing route 37A.

370A Ockendon Station – Grays or Purfleet Station route withdrawn, covered by 328.

370A New route Purfleet Station – Tilbury Ferry via Grays and Chadwell St Mary (works journeys).

371 Rainham – Grays via Wennington and West Thurrock extended from Grays to Tilbury (Feenan Highway) via Dock Road replacing route 31.

371A Purfleet Station – Grays via West Thurrock extended from Grays to Tilbury (Feenan Highway) via Dock Road replacing route 31.

379 New route Tilbury Docks – Chadwell St Mary via Civic Square (works journeys) replacing route 37B.

380 New route Grays – Linford replacing route 45.

Passengers alight in Orsett Road, Grays from STL 500 working on local route 323B after the reorganisation. *Alan B. Cross*

STL 731 is seen on an inclement day in Tilbury prior to working a journey to Nutberry Corner in Grays on special route 357. The roof-box STL in the background is working on route 371. *Alan B. Cross*

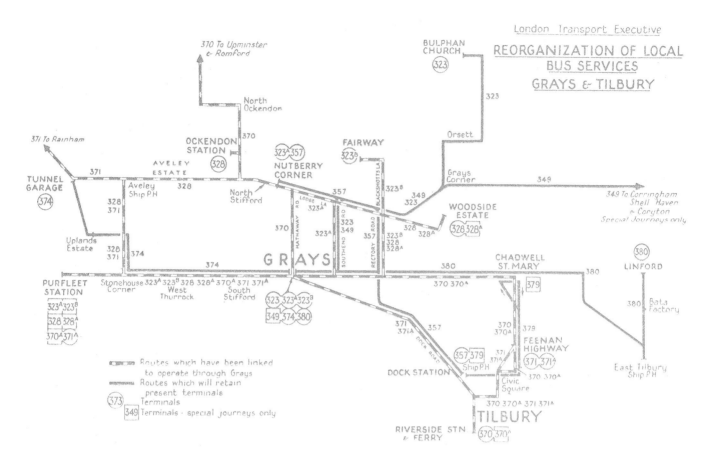

REORGANIZATION OF LOCAL BUS SERVICES GRAYS & TILBURY

The Grays reorganisation provided the restoration of through running from the west of Grays to Tilbury a facility used by many passengers and lost in 1934 when the planners got things so wrong. RT 4119 is seen at Grays Police Station on route 371 working from Rainham to Tilbury, Feenan Highway. *Alan B. Cross*

A publicly issued leaflet was produced which explained the reason for the changes, contained timetables, a route diagram and also showed boarding and alighting points in Grays town centre for LT and the remaining longer distance Eastern National and Westcliff routes. The only route in Grays to remain unaltered was the 374 to Aveley (Tunnel Garage) via Uplands Estate with positioning journeys to Rainham. Routes 367 and 368 were special services for Bata employees only. The special weekly tickets continued to be available for these two routes plus route 349. Routes 328/A, 370/A and the majority of 371/A were worked by RTs with STLs making up the balance. The Operating Manager's departmental meeting minutes recorded that the scheme proposed savings of 418 miles per week,

five vehicles and seven crews. The Country Area network had expanded considerably as Coryton was just nine miles from Southend as the crow flies. The timetables for the ex-Eastern National routes did appear in the North & North-East area staff timetable booklet for 26th September 1951 and although Grays remained administratively part of the North-East District of the Northern Division, the timetables for the routes were subsequently omitted from the staff timetable for that area and a separate Grays & Romford Area staff timetable was produced. The area continued to be isolated from the remainder of the Country Bus network and as will be seen, was to produce a considerable number of route alterations over the coming years mostly due to expansion of the LCC housing estate at Aveley.

F.H. Kilner (Transport) Ltd, one of the companies of the Hants & Sussex group, ceased to operate after 21st December 1954. In this 1952 view rebodied STL 1059 on route 434 bound for Horsham is seen at Crawley, The George, standing next to Hants & Sussex Bedford OB No. 151 working on route 33 to Horsham. *Alan B. Cross*

The Hants & Sussex Motor Services Ltd group of companies dated from 1937 and one of the companies, F.H. Kilner (Transport) Ltd, operated between Horsham and Roffey Corner both direct and via Littlehaven, between Horsham and Three Bridges via Roffey Corner, Faygate, Ifield and Crawley and between Horsham and Ewhurst via Oakwood Hill and Broadbridge Heath. In addition the company had recently started a service between Langley Green and Crawley with works projections to Manor Royal. Hants & Sussex was under-capitalised which led to the appointment of a receiver in December 1954 and the cessation of the above services after 21st December. It fell to the large companies to pick up the pieces with Aldershot & District, Southdown and London Transport providing services on short-term licences.

London Transport introduced route 852 between Three Bridges and Ewhurst via Horsham linking two of the former Hants & Sussex routes on 22nd December 1954. The situation was short-lived as following adverse comment from within the bus industry about expansion beyond its designated area, London Transport surrendered the section north of Horsham to Brown Motor Services on 18th May 1955. GS 81 is seen at Horsham, Carfax heading for Ewhurst. *Malcolm Papes collection*

London Transport introduced GS operated route 852 on 22nd December from Ewhurst to Three Bridges via Horsham thus linking up two of the routes. Certain journeys ran as 852A direct via the A264 rather than via Faygate Lane. The Langley Green operation was adequately covered by existing route 476 which had been the subject of an enhanced service on 15th December. The situation was to be short-lived as London Transport received adverse criticism from within the bus industry for operating outside its designated boundaries to the north west of Horsham. The debacle over the introduction of route 383 in 1948 as described in Volume One clearly had not been forgotten. From 18th May 1955 route 852 was withdrawn between Ewhurst and Horsham with this section passing to A.T. Brady's Brown Motor Services. The section via Littlehaven had been uncovered since the collapse but from 18th May 1955 new route 434A was provided between Horsham and Roffey Corner via Littlehaven with odd projections to Crawley Garage and one morning journey which started at Dormansland.

The origins of Lee & District went back to 1926 and by the mid-1950s was under the proprietorship of T.J. Brown. It operated outside the Special Area between Kings Ash and Chesham Broadway so could not be compulsorily acquired under the terms of the 1933 Act. When Mr. Brown's partnership had broken up in 1953 he sought to sell the service to London Transport which decided that if Brown stopped operating, it would provide a replacement. The service consisted of a trip for shoppers between Kings Ash and Chesham on Wednesday and Friday afternoons, but on Saturday and Sunday a more intensive service was run with some journeys starting at Swan Bottom instead of Kings Ash. From Lee Common the route was duplicated by the 394/A but many local people had remained loyal to the independent operator. Mr. Brown finally surrendered his licence and from 4th January 1956, London Transport provided a replacement service numbered 394D. It could be worked fairly economically as it did not require the use of any additional vehicles.

The old established company, Birch Brothers, one-time London independent operator and in the post-war period perhaps most famous for operating the 203 express service between King's Cross and Rushden, also operated a number of local services in the Hitchin, Luton, Welwyn Garden City triangle. A number of its services were withdrawn or curtailed as a result of the Suez Crisis in January 1957 and the company was clearly suffering from declining passengers on these rural routes one of which was the 205 from Welwyn Garden City to Luton via Codicote, Kimpton and Chiltern Green. After 7th April 1958 the route was withdrawn between Welwyn Garden City and Kimpton over which section London Transport introduced Monday to Friday peak hour route 315 worked by an RT from Hatfield Garage. The route was Kimpton (Coopers Hill) to Welwyn Garden City where it terminated at either the Railway Station, Tewin Road or Black Fan Road.

The old-established firm of Lee & District operated between Kings Ash and Chesham entirely outside the LPTB Special Area so could not be compulsorily acquired. Many passengers remained loyal to the independent operator. The proprietor surrendered his licence to operate and London Transport provided replacement service 394D from 4th January 1956. In this view Lee & District Bedford OB registration No. SMY 547 takes on a good load in Chesham. *John Gillham/Tony Peters/Alan B. Cross*

CHAPTER 4 DEVELOPMENTS 1954–1955

Snow always meant difficulties for Country Buses but a genuine effort was made to keep the services running in a period when public transport was considered an essential service rather than 'nice-to-do'. Swanley's RT 3870, just a few months old, has got into difficulties at Swanley whilst working on route 401 in December 1950 and is given a helping hand by passengers and council workmen. *Topfoto*

In 1954 the service car miles run by Country Buses peaked at 47.9 million, and in 1955 the number of passenger journeys peaked at 297 million. Passenger demand had started to decline on Central Buses and trolleybuses but the establishment of the new towns and new housing estates in the Country Area had offset the decline to some extent although a gradual reduction in the level of Sunday services was to set in. The Country Area was moving towards a standardised fleet of just four main vehicle types: RT, RF, RLH and GS. A new and what was destined to the last operating manager under London Transport auspices would be appointed. Staff shortage, however, was a problem that was here to stay with the situation being highlighted with a ban on overtime and rest-day working in the autumn of 1954.

The first revisions to services were made on 6th January 1954 when routes 356 Luton

– Flamstead, 376 Luton – Kensworth and works service 376A were converted from a mix of RT and RF operation to full RT operation. A new route, 372A, was introduced from Welwyn Garden City Station to Little Ganett via Ludwick Way and Cole Green Lane operated by one RT from Hatfield Garage. New housing development at Merrow was served by new route 408A from Guildford (Onslow Street Bus Station) to Merrow (Bushy Hill) which was worked by one RT. Passenger demand was falling on Sundays and this was reflected in the service when routes 490 Singlewell – Hartley Court and 490A Northumberland Bottom – Hartley Court were revised to operate between Gravesend and Hartley Court on Sundays as route 490. On 25th January route 393 Harlow – Hoddesdon was re-routed away from a section of Netteswell Road (which was eventually to become a footpath and cycle track) to run via First Avenue.

There were a few notorious locations where the snow would always be particularly bad, and one such was Dunstable Downs. T 782 has had to be abandoned due to heavy snow. , *R.K. Blencome*

On 6th January 1954 Luton routes 356 and 376/A were converted from a mixture of RT and RF operation to be entirely RT worked. In this view a few years earlier RT 4033 is seen in Luton working to Markyate on route 356. *Alan B. Cross*

GS 71 is seen in Hoddesdon taking on passengers on route 393 heading for Harlow. The route underwent some re-routeing in Harlow on 25th January 1954 as the new town gradually developed. *Alan B. Cross*

A new works route 392B was introduced on 3rd March 1954 between Stevenage, Caxton Way and Bedwell. Hitchin's mud spattered RT 3450 is seen at Stevenage, White Lion working on the route. The running number HN 109 denotes that it is a duplicate journey. *Alan B. Cross*

At this period London Transport's route numbering system was highly disciplined with numbers 1 to 299 being allocated to Central Buses, 301 to 499 to Country Buses, 500 and 600 series for trolleybuses and 700 series for Green Line Coaches. With the terrific expansion of the Country Area network since the war virtually all available numbers had been used up and new routes, particularly in the new towns, relied on the use of suffix letters. By March 1954 only the numbers 320 and 476 were available in the series. Interestingly the number 476 was the only one

that had not so far ever been used. It was therefore decided that an additional series would be employed starting at 801 in the northern area and 851 in the southern area. The London evening papers reported the change with headlines such as "London runs out of bus numbers". The revisions of 3rd March 1954 reflected the change:

314B New route Chaulden – Hemel Hempstead (Maylands Avenue) via Boxmoor Station, Two Waters, Marlowes and Adeyfield (works journeys). (RT)

392B New route Bedwell – Stevenage Industrial Area (Caxton Way) via Popple Way, Sish Lane, High Street, Bridge Road, Fairview Road Monday to Friday works journeys. (STL)

396A Harlow (Post Office) – The Dashes via First Avenue. Certain Monday to Saturday peak hour journeys now provided from Harlow Station to The Dashes via either London Road and First Avenue or Edinburgh Way and Howard Way. Harlow Station was the current Harlow Mill Station.

396B New route Potter Street – Mark Hall South via London Road, First Avenue and Howard Way. (RT)

801 New route Stevenage Station – Shephall via High Street, Great North Road, to Broadwater (The Roebuck) thence Shephall Lane. Certain Monday to Friday peak hour journeys re-routed via Bridge Road, Fairview Road, Gunnels Wood Road (as yet un-named) and Six Hills Way back to Great North Road. (RT)

RT 3723 is seen at Stevenage Station working on route 801 to Shephall. The route was introduced on 3rd March 1954 and was the first northern area route to be numbered in the 800 overspill series. The height of the roof at Hitchin Garage prevented double-deck vehicles from entering which led to obvious problems over bus washing. Eventually the roof was jacked up by the Works & Buildings department to allow double-deck buses to enter. *Alan B. Cross*

Crawley routes were subject to adjustment from 24th March 1954 with additional works journeys being provided on route 438 between Crawley and Gatwick Airport. The supplementary service on route 426 had school journeys provided between Ifield and Crossways (Hazlewick School) and on route 483 certain journeys were extended from Northgate to Crossways (Hazlewick School).

Prior to the introduction of the summer programme in May a number of timetable revisions in the North & North East area including Grays were made on 21st April 1954 which resulted in the following changes:

332 Aveley (Hall Road) – Aveley LCC Estate (Eskley Gardens) via Foyle Drive, Darenth Drive and Daiglen Drive also works journeys Purfleet Station – Eskley Gardens. Main route withdrawn (see 332A) now Purfleet Station – Aveley Estate (Eskley Gardens) works journeys. Note reference to LCC Estate now discontinued.

332A New route Aveley Estate (Usk Road) – Aveley Estate (Eskley Gardens) replacing route 332 main service. Odd journeys projected to Aveley Estate (Humber Avenue) and one journey from Ockendon Station to Usk Road via Ford Place. (RT)

332B New route Aveley Estate (Usk Road) – Purfleet Station or East Purfleet (Mill Road) positioning journeys. (RT)

368 Grays – Bata Shoe Factory via Chadwell Road (special Journeys) with certain journeys

running via Southend Road, Socketts Heath and Woodview instead of Chadwell Road direct. One journey now re-routed via Hathaway Road.

370 Romford – Tilbury Ferry. Projected in Romford to London Road Garage.

371B New route Grays – Aveley Estate (Usk Road) via West Thurrock. Monday to Friday odd journeys and Saturday afternoon. (RT)

389 Hertford – Sawbridgeworth. Odd projection to and from Horns Mill withdrawn on conversion of route from T to GS operation.

Route 389 was converted from T to GS operation on 21st April 1954 and was not officially allocated the RF type. In this view at Hertford Bus Station RF 563 is seen standing in for a T sometime before the conversion.
Ron Wellings

On 21st April 1954 a new route 332A was introduced from the west part of Aveley Estate at Usk Road to the main estate at Eskley Gardens. RT 3634 is seen on the Usk Road terminal working. In a scene no doubt considered abhorrent in today's health and safety society, children play in the yet to be finished road, and were no doubt none the worse for the experience.
Alan B. Cross

On 19th May 1954 the single-deck bus position was eased when route 318 lost its RFs in favour of RT operation. In this view outside the Malden Hotel at Watford Junction RF 603 takes on a good load whilst heading for Abbots Langley. The conductor is in the usual position when passengers were boarding or alighting – pressed up against the windscreen. There was simply nowhere else to stand. A Cravens bodied RT on route 385 is seen in the background.

With the introduction of the main summer programme on 19th May 1954 the following changes applied:

301D New route Watford Junction – Ovaltine Works via Watford By-Pass (works journeys). (RT/STL)

305A Gerrards Cross – Chalfont Common. Certain Saturday journeys projected to Horne Hill.

317A New route Hemel Hempstead – Nettleden – Little Gaddesden (319 renumbered). (T)

318 Chipperfield – Abbots Langley – Watford – Sarratt or Bucks Hill. Converted from RF to RT operation and revised to run Abbots Langley (Hazelwood Lane) – Watford – Sarratt with projections to Chipperfield.

318A Two Waters – Kings Langley Station – Abbots Langley – Watford (works journeys) renumbered 319A.

318A New route Abbots Langley (Hazelwood Lane) – Watford – Bucks Hill. (RT)

318B Two Waters – Kings Langley – Chipperfield – (positioning journeys) renumbered 319B and projected to Sarratt.

318C Watford via Garston (in that direction only) then Kings Langley Station – Two Waters via Ovaltine Works and Apsley Mills (journeys only) renumbered 319C and slightly revised.

318D Watford (Clarendon Corner) – Langleybury School via Garston and Abbots Langley. One journey returning from Langleybury School is projected from Watford to Sarratt, renumbered 319D and its Sarratt projection withdrawn.

319 Hemel Hempstead – Nettleden – Little Gaddesden renumbered 317A.

319 New route Chipperfield – Abbots Langley – Watford with projections from Sarratt to Chipperfield replacing part of old route 318. (RF)

319A New route Two Waters – Nash Mills – Kings Langley Station – Abbots Langley – Watford (works journeys) formerly 318A. (RF)

319B New route Two Waters – Kings Langley – Chipperfield – Sarratt (positioning journeys) formerly 318B. (RF)

319C New route Watford via Garston and Kings Langley Station (in that direction only) then Ovaltine Works – Apsley Mills – Two Waters (works journeys) ex 318C. (RF)

319D New school route Watford (Clarendon Corner) – Langleybury School via Garston and Abbots Langley ex 318D. (RF)

325 Townsend (Batchwood Drive) – Cottonmill Estate (Abbots Avenue). Extended from Townsend to New Greens Estate (High Oaks) and loop working introduced in Cottonmill Estate. Two routeings observed as follows: New Greens Estate – Townsend (Becketts Avenue, Langley Crescent) – St Peters Street – Prospect Road – Abbots Avenue – Maynards Drive – St Peters Street – thence to New Greens Estate via outward route; or New Greens Estate – Townsend (Batchwood Drive, Waverley Road) – St Peters Street – Maynards Drive – Abbots Avenue – Prospect Road – St Peters Street – thence to New Greens Estate via outward route.

326 Sands (works journeys) – High Wycombe (Mill End Road) – Micklefield Estate (Buckingham Drive). Extended in Micklefield Estate to Woodside Road.

347A New route Watford – Hemel Hempstead (Maylands Avenue) via Garston (works journeys). (RT)

355 Borehamwood (Cowley Hill) – St Albans (Lancaster Road) via Radlett. Extended from Lancaster Road to Beech Road.

391 Harpenden – Wheathampstead – St Albans – Hill End Hospital with projections to Hill End Station or Tyttenhanger. Short journeys between Harpenden and Batford Mill projected to Batford Estate.

391A New Greens Estate (Woollam Crescent) – St Albans – Hill End Hospital with projections to Hill End Station or Tyttenhanger. Re-routed in Townsend via Batchwood Drive, Waverley Road instead of Becketts Avenue, Langley Crescent.

422 Leatherhead – Boxhill. One journey intermediately re-routed via route 435 to serve Headley Court RAF Hospital.

476 New route Crawley – Langley Green (anti-clockwise loop via Martyrs Avenue, returning via Langley Drive). (RT)

The revisions to the 318 group appear to be complicated – basically the main service between Abbots Langley and Sarratt or Bucks Hill was converted from RF to RT and all journeys beyond Abbots Langley towards Kings Langley Station were renumbered from the 318 group to a new 319 group. Route 313 was seasonally extended to Whipsnade Zoo and route 474 re-introduced.

In a complicated renumbering exercise with the 19th May 1954 changes all the 318 suffix routes became 319 suffix routes. T 785 is seen entering Two Waters Garage before the change on the old route 318A. *Alan B. Cross*

Above left: The existing route 319 between Hemel Hempstead and Little Gaddesden was renumbered 317A in the 19th May 1954 changes. T 780 is seen working on route 319 sometime before the revision. *John Herting collection*

Above: The complicated route changes of 19th May 1954 saw a new route 319 running from Watford to Sarratt via Abbots Langley. The destination blind on RF 602 indicates the indirect nature of the route. *Ron Wellings*

Left: The new towns were starting to grow up – on 19th May 1954 route 476 was introduced between Crawley and Langley Green. RT 3676 appears to doing good business on the new route. Interestingly the route number 476 had never previously been used by Country Buses. *Alan B. Cross*

The first route number in the southern area 850 series was used on 30th May 1954 when 851 was introduced as a special hospital service from Three Bridges Station to Smallfield Hospital. RT 3619 rests in Crawley Garage. *Alan B. Cross*

Once modifications had been made by the local authority to a railway bridge just one RLH type was allocated to route 447 for short workings between Redhill and South Merstham. RLH 41 is seen on the stand in Redhill. *Alan B. Cross*

On 11th August 1954 the shuttle service on route 426 between Ifield and Three Bridges which had been introduced on 13th June 1951 was sensibly renumbered 426A. In this view taken in 1956 red RT 767 has been loaned to Crawley, probably over a summer weekend and is seen at Crawley, The George next to a Southdown bus. The running number CY 202 indicates a duplicate working – in 1956 duplicates were renumbered from the 100 series to the 200 series. *Alan B. Cross/ Roy Hobbs*

On 30th May the first Southern area route in the 850 series, 851 was introduced between Three Bridges Station and Smallfield Hospital on Sunday only for hospital visitors, worked by one RT. On 7th July one RLH was allocated to the 447 group for workings between Redhill and South Merstham. Two new routes appeared on 11th August when one early journey on route 407 between Windsor and Slough Trading Estate was intermediately re-routed via Stoke Road, Elliman Avenue and Whitby Road and numbered 407B. There was no return working. Sensibly the route 426 RT-worked shuttle service between Ifield and Three Bridges was renumbered 426A.

A further fares revision applied from 26th September 1954 when 3½d and 8½d fares were increased by a halfpenny and 5d and 10d fares were increased by a penny. The usual exemptions applied where other operators' fare scales were in use. The Crown Road to Brentwood return on route 339 was withdrawn leaving the Ongar to Brentwood return fare the only one remaining on the network.

This fares revision came at a rather inopportune time for London Transport as there was a continual worsening of the staff shortage problem. An unofficial ban on overtime and rest-day working by drivers and conductors had been observed since mid-August. Staff shortage was an acute problem in the Central Area but the ban did affect services from some Country Area garages where staff shortage was a problem. The result was that buses were withdrawn when staff were not available and journeys were cut. The public was appalled at the situation which exposed the fact that services were kept going only by the vast amount of overtime and rest-day working being performed by the crews. The winter programme was planned to apply from 6th October 1954 but it is possible that in the general confusion some changes were deferred for a week or fortnight. Staff shortage was particularly acute at Amersham Garage and from 6th October emergency cuts were imposed on routes 305/A, 336, 353, 359 and 362/A. In addition cuts were made on route 418 and a number of Green Line routes. The imposition of similar cuts in the Central Area resulted in unofficial strike action. The ban on overtime and rest-day working was called off on 20th October and all emergency schedules were cancelled. Permanent reductions were made to the service on routes 305/A and 353 from 15th December.

RF 567 takes on passengers at Hertford Bus Station prior to working to Lemsford Lane in Welwyn Garden City. Route 372 had been started by Leyland Cubs in 1948 and was the subject of a number of minor changes in Welwyn Garden City as services in the area developed. *Ron Wellings*

This Bedford coach, TNO 57, owned by Ongar Motors is seen at the Harlow Post Office stand working on route 396. It is believed that the coach was used during the crews' ban on overtime and rest day working in autumn 1954. *Alan B. Cross*

The route changes planned for 6th October 1954 were as follows:

314B Chaulden – Hemel Hempstead (Maylands Avenue) (works journeys) route withdrawn, covered by 320.

316 Chesham – Hemel Hempstead (High Street Green). Curtailed at Hemel Hempstead (The Parade).

320 New route Leverstock Green – Warners End (Martindale Road) via Leverstock Green Road, Adeyfield Road, Marlowes, Two Waters, Boxmoor station and Northridge Way. Certain journeys were re-routed away from Leverstock Green Road via Maylands Avenue and Wood Lane End to serve the industrial area. (RT)

338 Harperbury Hospital – St Albans with projection to Sandridge. Extended from Harperbury Hospital to Radlett Station.

347 Boxmoor Station – Uxbridge. Withdrawn between Boxmoor Station and Hemel Hempstead (The Parade) due to the re-introduction of route 320.

372 Hertford – Welwyn Garden City (Lemsford Lane). Re-routed away from Cole Green Lane and Ludwick Way to run via Heronswood Road. Wheatley Road short journeys now terminate at Great Ganett. Sunday service withdrawn between Welwyn Garden City Station and Lemsford Lane (see route 372A).

372A Welwyn Garden City Station – Little Ganett via Ludwick Way and Cole Green Lane. Revised to terminate at Great Ganett and Sunday service provided between Lemsford Lane and Great Ganett. Note: Little Ganet terminus has now been redefined Great Ganett.

392 Stevenage Station to Monks Wood via Sish Lane direct. Certain garage journeys now work in service to and from Hitchin (St Mary's Square or Garage).

392A Stevenage Station to Bedwell via Haycroft Road, Greydells Road, Poppleway and Bedwell Crescent. One journey each way on Monday to Friday Stevenage Station – Monks Wood for schools requirements. Now extended Monday to Friday except at peak periods, Saturday early am and evening and Sunday from Bedwell Crescent to Marymead via Colestrete, Six Hills Way, Valley Way and Broadwater Crescent. Certain garage journeys work in service to and from Hitchin (St Mary's Square or Garage).

392C New route Saturday only Stevenage Station (morning) or Hitchin (St Mary's Square) (afternoon) – Marymead via Sish Lane direct thence as 392A. (RT) Note routes 392A and 392C were subsequently extended from Marymead to Longmeadow on 15th December.

396A Harlow (Post Office) – The Dashes via First Avenue. Certain Monday to Saturday peak hour journeys provided from Harlow Station to The Dashes via either London Road and First Avenue or Edinburgh Way and Howard Way. Now revised to run from Harlow Station to Fourth Avenue via London Road and First Avenue daily retaining peak hour journeys via Edinburgh Way and Howard Way. Certain journeys on route 396 from either Epping or Bishop's Stortford were also projected to Fourth Avenue.

396B Potter Street – Mark Hall South via London Road, First Avenue and Howard Way. Certain peak hour journeys introduced between Potter Street and Edinburgh Way via London Road, Second Avenue and Howard Way.

415 Guildford – Ripley. Certain Monday to Saturday journeys projected to Ockham.

423A Dartford – Joyce Green Hospital – Wells Factory. Certain journeys extended to Watchgate (Hill Rise).

423B Littlebrook Power Station – Watchgate (Lanes End) works journeys. Extended to Watchgate (Hill Rise).

423C New route Littlebrook Power Station – Dartford Heath works journey in that direction only. Last day of operation 25th January 1955.

438 Crawley Down – Crawley (works service). Journey provided from Three Bridges to Gatwick Airport via Crawley.

467A New route Sunday pm only Dartford (Bow Arrow Lane) – Wilmington or Horton Kirby replacing route 499 on that day. (RT)

498 Gravesend (Clock Tower) – Coldharbour Estate. Certain journeys re-routed at Kent & Essex P.H. to run via Dover Road to Northfleet (Plough).

RT 3473 is seen on route 392 at Monks Wood terminus in Stevenage against a background of unfinished houses. The bus carries SV stencil plates which denotes that it is working from the temporary premises in Fishers Green Road which opened in October 1955. Although the bus is in green livery it inexplicably carries a rear offside route plate.
John Shearman

Saturday only route 392C was introduced on 9th October 1954 running between Stevenage Station or Hitchin and Marymead. RT 3725 is seen at the then Stevenage Station and the destination blind provides for a lazy display. The very informative intermediate points blind incorrectly shows the route 392A display. *Ron Wellings*

In addition the seasonal adjustments were made to routes 313 and 474. In consequence of the enhancements to route 392A and the introduction of route 392C the service on route 801 (Stevenage Station – Shephall) was reduced from daily to Monday to Friday peak periods with most journeys running via Gunnels Wood Road. Some further alterations applied to Stevenage works services from 17th November when route 303B Hitchin – Stevenage (Broomin Green) was revised to run between Hitchin Station and Six Hills Way via either White Lion or Stevenage Station and Caxton Way or Gunnels Wood Road. Route 392B Bedwell – Caxton Way was extended to Six Hills Way via either Caxton Way or Gunnels Wood Road. New RT operated works route 801A linked Stevenage Station and

Marymead via High Street, Great North Road, Shephall Lane and Broadwater Crescent. Certain journeys were re-routed via Bridge Road, Fairview Road, Gunnels Wood Road and Six Hills Way back to Great North Road. The route was subsequently extended from Marymead to Longmeadow on 15th December.

The use of route numbers 431B (Knockholt Pound – Fort Halstead) and 431C (Knockholt Station – Fort Halstead) was, as far as can be established, discontinued from 15th November 1954. The journeys continued to operate un-numbered being classed as "Fort Halstead Works Journeys". It is unclear what the purpose of this change might have been but the use of the route numbers had certainly been reinstated by May 1959.

Below left: On 6th October 1954 route 415 gained what was to be a short-lived extension through previously unserved roads from Ripley to Ockham. RT 3171 lays over outside Guildford Garage between trips. *Vectis Transport Publications*

Below: In 1955 a number of Cravens bodied RTs were sent from the Central Area to work at various Country Area garages. RT 1520 is seen crossing the railway bridge of the Westerham branch at Dunton Green while running as a Fort Halstead Works Special to Sevenoaks. *Alan B. Cross/W.R. Legg*

New off peak route 388A was introduced on 15th December 1954 running between Hertford Bus Station and Sele Farm Estate. GS 73 on route 388A stands alongside GS 18 on the parent route 388 heading for Welwyn.

Further service revisions were implemented on 15th December 1954 as follows:

310 Hertford North Station – Enfield Town. Certain Monday to Saturday journeys extended from Hertford North Station to Sele Farm Estate (Windsor Drive). See also route 388A.

326 Sands (works journeys) – High Wycombe (Mill End Road) – Micklefield Estate (Woodside Road). Journeys to New Bowerdean Road formerly 326A now run as 326. Certain journeys to and from Micklefield Estate run direct via Easton Street and London Road instead of Totteridge Road and Bowerdean Road. Note Thames Valley retained the route number 26A for its New Bowerdean Road service.

326A Sands (works journeys) – High Wycombe (Mill End Road) – New Bowerdean route renumbered 326.

388A New route Hertford (Bus Station) – Sele Farm Estate (Windsor Drive) Monday to Friday off-peak periods. (GS) Service provided by route 310 at other times.

405 West Croydon – Crawley with projections to Three Bridges and Goffs Park. Crawley terminus changed from The George to The Boulevard with certain exceptions.

476 Crawley – Langley Green. Crawley terminus changed from The George to The Boulevard.

483 Crawley – Northgate (Midgeley Road) with schools projections to Crossways. Crawley terminus changed from The George to The Boulevard.

851 Three Bridges Station and Smallfield Hospital (hospital service). Re-routed away from Tinsley Green to run via London Road and Povey Cross and additional stops provided.

The revision to routes 326/A had originally been proposed for 6th October and involved London Transport handing over the entire New Bowerdean Road service to Thames Valley. Clearly agreement failed to be reached between the two operators and the above proposal represented an acceptable compromise. The change of terminal in Crawley represented the first stage of the relocation to the new town centre prior to the opening of the bus station. Routes 426, 426A, 434, 438 group and 473 continued to operate to The George as previously.

The question of staff shortage was to continue to be a thorn in the side of London Transport for the years to come. Despite various initiatives to overcome the problem the situation was destined to become progressively worse. London Transport had opened a hostel for male staff at The Grove near Watford, the war-time headquarters of the London Midland and Scottish Railway. Hostels were established for female staff at Hertford, Windsor and Weybridge (for nearby Addlestone Garage). The Hertford hostel was only in use from 1956 to 1958. London Transport recruited staff from the provinces and Ireland as drivers and conductors with the added incentive of the provision of accommodation.

The use of the route number 326A was discontinued on 15th December 1954 when the journeys to and from New Bowerdean Road were run as 326. RT 3445 is seen taking on passengers in High Wycombe before the change.
Alan B. Cross

The low-height RLHs were a familiar sight in the south-west corner of the network on a number of routes worked by Addlestone and Guildford garages. One of the original batch, RLH 12 is seen at Onslow Street Bus Station in Guildford working on route 463 to Walton.

Harlow New Town local route 396A was extended to Hare Street on 26th January 1955. RT 1017 stands at Harlow Post Office prior to working a journey to Hare Street. *C. Carter*

On 12th January 1955 route 371B was revised to operate between Rainham and Tilbury via Mill Road at Aveley with certain journeys starting from Aveley Usk Road. RT 4115 is seen on the route heading for Tilbury, Feenan Highway in 1958. *Alan B. Cross*

Mr B.H. Harbour, the Operating Manager (Country Buses & Coaches), who had succeeded the original holder of that post and founder of East Surrey, Mr A.H. Hawkins, in 1946, was appointed a full-time member of the London Transport Executive in October 1954. The post of Operating Manager (Country Buses & Coaches) was filled by Mr Geoffrey Fernyhough then aged 44 who at one time held the post of Divisional Superintendent (North). A somewhat charismatic figure, Mr Fernyhough had commenced his career with the LGOC in 1930 and transferred to Country Buses in 1935, later becoming a District Superintendent. He served during the Second World War with the Royal Artillery gaining the rank of lieutenant-colonel. After a further spell in Central Buses he was involved with the establishment of the Central Distribution Services organisation in 1949 becoming its first Superintendent before returning to Country Buses. The organisation of

the department was explained in a Traffic Circular upon the appointment of Mr Fernyhough. There was a headquarters, a Northern Division based at St Albans and a Southern Division based at Reigate. Each divisional superintendent had an assistant. The Northern Division was divided into three districts, North West, North and North East, and the southern division was divided into four districts, South West, South, South East and Central, the latter being responsible for Green Line coach operation in London. At this time High Wycombe Garage was transferred from the South West district to the North West district.

The following alterations took place in the Grays area on 12th January 1955:

328C Aveley Estate (Elan Road) – Rainham via Aveley High Street, Purfleet Road and Wennington. Re-routed away from Purfleet Road to run via Mill Road and Sandy Lane to provide an improved service to the west side of Aveley Estate. Saturday peak hour journeys added.

332B Aveley Estate (Usk Road) – Purfleet Station or East Purfleet (Mill Road) positioning journeys. Service reduced to just one journey from Usk Road to Purfleet Station (in that direction only).

371B Grays – Aveley Estate (Usk Road) via West Thurrock, Monday to Friday odd journeys and Saturday afternoon. Revised to operate between Tilbury (Feenan Highway) and Rainham via Dock Road, West Thurrock, Aveley, Mill Road, Sandy Lane and Wennington daily. Odd journeys and Saturday afternoon service Tilbury to Aveley Estate (Usk Road).

374 Grays – Uplands Estate – Aveley (Tunnel Garage) with projections to Rainham and a limited Sunday service from Tilbury (Feenan Highway) – Uplands Estate via Dock Road and Grays. Revised on Sunday to run between Grays and Uplands Estate.

A new RT worked school route, 334A, was introduced on 26th January 1955 running from Two Waters Garage to High Street Green via Durrants Hill Road, Barnacres Road, Bennetts End Road, Longlands and Adeyfield Road. Certain journeys for school traffic on route 372 (Hertford – Welwyn Garden City) were re-routed away from Heronswood Road to run via Cole Green Lane and Ludwick Way as 372A. In Harlow New Town route 393 was re-routed between Fourth Avenue and Linford End to run via Harberts Road from the same date and route 396/A was extended from the Fourth Avenue terminus to Hare Street.

On 2nd February 1955 the following alterations to Crawley works services took place:

438B New route Crawley Down – Crawley (George) via Copthorne, Tinsley Green, Gatwick Airport (Old) Station and Manor Royal. (RT)

438C New route East Grinstead – Crawley (George) via Snow Hill or Crawley Down thence Copthorne, Ridleys Corner, Tinsley Green, Gatwick Airport Stn and Manor Royal. (RT)

476A New works route Langley Green – Three Bridges Station via Langley Drive (return Martyrs Avenue), Manor Royal, Gatwick Road and North Road. (RT)

853 New works route Three Bridges Station circular via North Road, Gatwick Road, Manor Royal, London Road and Three Bridges Road. Service fragmented with few through journeys. (RT)

In consequence of these changes the supplementary service on route 405 between Three Bridges and Manor Royal (Faraday Road) was withdrawn and works route 438A lost its journeys via Crawley Down.

Part of the summer programme for 1955 was introduced on 18th May when the following route alterations were made:

305 Gerrards Cross – Beaconsfield via The Chalfonts with certain journeys via Gold Hill Common (Leachcroft Estate). Extended from Gerrards Cross to Uxbridge and garage journeys worked in service to and from Amersham.

305A Gerrards Cross – Chalfont Common with certain journeys via Gold Hill Common (Leachcroft Estate) and certain Saturday journeys projected to Horne Hill. Extended from Gerrards Cross to Uxbridge.

319C Watford via Garston and Kings Langley Station (in that direction only) then Ovaltine Works – Apsley Mills – Two Waters (works journeys). The journey from Watford projected from Two Waters Garage to Hemel Hempstead (Parade).

339 Epping or Coxtie Green – Warley. Certain short journeys from the Brentwood direction terminating at Ongar Station extended to Shelley (Red Cow).

378 Boxmoor (Wharf Road) – Apsley Mills works journeys. Part of service revised to start from Warners End (Martindale Road) via Northridge Way.

419 Langley Vale – Epsom (Brettgrave) permanently converted from RF crew to RF one-man operation after an earlier experiment.

434A New route Roffey Corner – Horsham via Littlehaven with odd projections to Crawley Garage and one morning journey which started at Dormansland. This route replaced the service previously operated by F.H. Kilner (Transport) Ltd until the failure of the company in December 1954.

473 Edenbridge – Horsham via Rowfant. Re-routed away from Crawley Lane, east of Three Bridges to run via Worth Road.

493 Englefield Green (Larchwood Drive) – Botleys Park (St Peters Hospital) (hospital service). Intermediately re-routed away from a section of Stroude Road via Pooley Green Road, Thorpe Lea Road and Wickham Lane and two additional stops provided.

852 Three Bridges – Ewhurst via Faygate and Horsham. Revised to operate between Crawley Garage and Horsham.

In addition route 313 was seasonally extended to Whipsnade Zoo but Sunday only route 474 from Slough to Burnham Beeches was not re-introduced until 17th July.

A further fares revision applied from 5th June 1955 when all fares of 7d or over were increased by 1d. Early morning single fares were also increased by 1d, with the scale now ranging from 5d to 1s. On a number of routes certain fares that remained unaltered at this time were similarly increased on 18th September. Falling leisure traffic was having an effect on receipts, particularly on Sundays, and two initiatives were introduced from 26th June 1955 in an attempt to stem the tide. On Sundays a maximum cheap fare was imposed on certain routes during the summer season for all journeys commencing before 1pm. The routes concerned were 335, 353, 370, 401, 408 and 470 plus sections only on routes 306 (Bushey Heath – New Barnet), 403 (Wallington – Sevenoaks) and 441 (Windsor – High Wycombe). The maximum fare varied from route to route ranging from 8d on 306 to 1s 9d on 408 and 470.

On 2nd February 1955 the supplementary service on route 405 between Three Bridges and Manor Royal was replaced by new route 853. Red RT 853 is seen at Manor Royal with new factory buildings in the background in July 1956. *Alan B. Cross/Roy Hobbs*

GS 81 is seen working on route 852 after it lost the projection to Three Bridges on 18th May 1955. *J. Gillham/Tony Peters*

CHEAP SUMMER
SUNDAY MORNING FARES
ON GREEN BUS ROUTES OF
LONDON TRANSPORT

On the Country Bus Routes shown below you can travel ANY DISTANCE on Summer Sunday mornings between the points stated for a new Cheap Maximum Fare. You must start your journey *before 1 p.m.* For distances costing less than the Cheap Maximum Fare you pay ordinary fare. Children travel at half fare.

Bus 306	(between NEW BARNET STN. and BUSHEY HEATH only)	Max. fare 8d.
Bus 335	WATFORD - WINDSOR	Max. fare 1/7
Bus 353	BERKHAMSTED - WINDSOR	Max. fare 1/7
Bus 370	ROMFORD - TILBURY	Max. fare 1/1
Bus 401	BELVEDERE - SEVENOAKS	Max. fare 1/6
Bus 403	(between WALLINGTON and SEVENOAKS only)	Max. fare 1/6
Bus 408	CHELSHAM - GUILDFORD	Max. fare 1/9
Bus 441	(between HIGH WYCOMBE and WINDSOR only)	Max. fare 1/-
Bus 470	CHELSHAM - DORKING	Max. fare 1/9

For times of buses ask at your nearest Country Bus Garage or Enquiry Office.

MAKE THE MOST OF YOUR PUBLIC TRANSPORT

655 1377 ML 5m   1250 Bournehall Press Ltd., Bushey

The main service on route 424 between East Grinstead and Reigate lost its RF allocation for RTs on 16th May 1956. RF 671 is seen in East Grinstead heading for Reigate some time before the change. The 424 shuttle journeys between Horley and Horne or Outwood Common continued to be single-deck worked. *W.J. Haynes*

The second initiative was the issue of rail-road return tickets on summer Sundays from certain stations on the Underground to Windsor via Uxbridge and buses 457/A. The tickets were issued at all stations between Willesden Green and Hillingdon on the Metropolitan and Bakerloo lines and also between North Ealing and South Harrow on the Piccadilly Line.

The remainder of the summer programme was introduced on 13th July as follows:

310 Hertford (Sele Farm Estate) – Enfield Town. Extended in Sele Farm Estate from Windsor Drive to Police Cottages.

330 St Albans – Welwyn Garden City (Cole Green Lane). Certain journeys extended in Welwyn Garden City to Howlands via Hollybush Lane.

343 St Albans (Marshalswick) – Welham Green. Extended from Welham Green to Brookmans Park Station.

350 Hertford – Bishop's Stortford via Wareside with certain journeys projected in Hertford to Horns Mill. One journey projected to Sele Farm Estate.

355 Borehamwood (Cowley Hill) – St Albans (Beech Road) via Radlett. Sunday am journey projected to Sandridge.

384B Walkern – Letchworth via Letchworth Gate (works journeys). Journey provided to start from Benington.

392A Stevenage Station to Longmeadow via Haycroft Road, Greydells Road, Poppleway, Bedwell Crescent, Colestrete and Valley Way. Certain garage journeys work in service to and from Hitchin (St Mary's Square or Garage). Now re-routed away from Longmeadow to a new terminus, Hydean Way (Peartree Way).

392C Saturday only Stevenage Station (morning) or Hitchin (St Mary's Square) (afternoon) – Longmeadow via Sish Lane direct thence as 392A. Now re-routed away from Longmeadow to a new terminus, Hydean Way (Peartree Way).

801A Stevenage Station and Longmeadow via High Street, Great North Road, Shephall Lane and Broadwater Crescent. Certain journeys re-routed via Bridge Road, Fairview Road, Gunnels Wood Road and Six Hills Way back to Great North Road (works journeys). Now made a daily service replacing routes 392A/C to Longmeadow. Certain journeys and Saturdays, except evenings, projected to and from Hitchin (St Mary's Square).

802 New route Stevenage (Hydean Way, Peartree Way) – Six Hills Way via Colestrete, Bedwell Crescent, Monks Wood, Elder Road, Great North Road, Caxton Way and Gunnels Wood Road (loop). Some journeys do not run via the Caxton Way and Gunnels Wood Road loop working (works journeys). (RT)

A new lay-by for services terminating on the west side of Welwyn Garden City Station was opened on 17th July 1955.

In some town centres where there was not a conveniently located garage London Transport provided enquiry office and waiting room facilities. This one in New Road Gravesend had a bus and coach stop located outside. *London Transport Museum*

Route 466A from Englefield Green to Knowle Hill was withdrawn with the winter programme for 1955 which came into operation on 5th October. Just four days prior to the withdrawal, RF 641 is seen at Egham heading for Knowle Hill. *Alan B. Cross*

The winter programme applied from 5th October 1955 when the following route changes were made:

323A Purfleet Station (works journeys) – Grays – Nutberry Corner. Service now reduced to peak hours, lunch time and odd journeys. Journey from Tank Hill transferred to 323B. The extension of route 323B was felt adequate to serve the Nutberry Corner catchment area.

323B Purfleet Station (works journeys) – Grays – Fairway. Extended from Fairway to Stifford Clays via Crammavill Street and Whitmore Avenue. Journey from Hedleys Works provided.

324A New route Aveley Estate (Eskley Gardens) – Woodside Estate (Buxton Road) via Daiglen Drive, Darenth Lane, Foyle Drive, North Stifford and Grays. Sunday only operation replacing routes 324 and 328 on that day. (RT)

340A Potters Bar – Hatfield Garage (school service for Hatfield Technical College). Revised in Hatfield to serve Hazelgrove School via Cavendish Way and Bishops Rise on or about this date.

350 Hertford – Bishop's Stortford via Wareside with certain journeys projected in Hertford to Horns Mill. One journey projected to Sele Farm Estate. Now extended in Bishop's Stortford from Southmill Road to Havers Lane Estate.

350A Hertford – Bishop's Stortford via Stanstead Abbots with certain journeys projected in Hertford to Horns Mill. Now extended in Bishop's Stortford from Southmill Road to Havers Lane Estate.

392 Hitchin or Stevenage Station to Monks Wood via Sish Lane direct. Re-routed away from Sish Lane to run via Haycroft Road and Greydells Road.

392A Hitchin or Stevenage Station – Hydean Way (Peartree Way) via Haycroft Road, Greydells Road, Poppleway, Bedwell Crescent, Colestrete and Valley Way. Re-routed away from Haycroft Road and Greydells Road to run via Sish Lane direct. Saturday afternoon journeys provided to and from Hitchin (St Mary's Square) – previously provided by route 392C.

392B Bedwell – Stevenage Industrial Area (Six Hills Way) via Popple Way, Sish Lane, High Street, Bridge Road, Fairview Road (works journeys) route withdrawn, replaced by 802.

392C Saturday only Stevenage Station (morning) or Hitchin (St Mary's Square) (afternoon) – Hydean Way (Peartree Way) via Sish Lane direct thence as 392A. Route withdrawn and covered by re-routed 392A.

393 Harlow (Green Man) – Hoddesdon (Middlefield Road). Intermediately re-routed between Netteswell Cross and Harlow (Post Office) via School Lane and First Avenue. Netteswell Road reduced to cycle track and footpath.

412 Dorking North Station – Holmbury St Mary (Sutton) or Leith Hill. Section from Parkhurst Corner to Leith Hill withdrawn.

424 Due to reduction in main service on Sunday between Reigate and East Grinstead variant journeys via Duxhurst and Snow Hill withdrawn.

441 Staines Central Station – High Wycombe or Hedgerley Village. Certain journeys from the Windsor direction projected to Old Windsor Hospital via Crimp Hill. Old Windsor Hospital was previously designated Windsor Emergency Hospital.

463A Walton – Ripley (Sunday pm only) route withdrawn, covered by reinstatement of full Sunday service on route 436A.

466A Englefield Green (Larchwood Drive) – Knowle Hill route withdrawn.

473 Edenbridge – Horsham via Rowfant. School journey from Crawley direction projected to Blackwell County Primary School in East Grinstead.

476 Crawley (The Boulevard) – Langley Green. Odd journey projected from Crawley to Three Bridges Station via Three Bridges Road.

490 Singlewell – Hartley Court via Southfleet and New Barn. Withdrawn between Singlewell and Gravesend (Clock Tower).

490A Northumberland Bottom – Hartley Court via Southfleet and New Barn route withdrawn, covered by 490.

802 Stevenage (Hydean Way, Peartree Way) – Six Hills Way via Colestrete, Bedwell Crescent, Monks Wood, Elder Way, Great North Road, Caxton Way and Gunnels Wood Road (loop). Supplementary circular service introduced in place of route 392B from Bedwell via Popple Way, Sish Lane, Bridge Road, Fairview Road, Caxton Way, Six Hills Way, Great North Road, Elder Way and Monks Wood with certain journeys projected from Bedwell to Hydean Way.

The temporary garage in Fishers Green Road, Stevenage helped to relieve pressure on the overcrowded shed at Hitchin until a brand new garage replaced both and catered for New Town services. The temporary premises provided six buses and four coaches for service. *Ken Glazier*

The usual seasonal alteration to route 313 and withdrawal of route 474 took place. On the date of this revision the pressure on the small Hitchin Garage and its rented yard was relieved a little when temporary premises were opened in Fishers Green Road, Stevenage (coded SV). The former requirement of 27 vehicles, including Green Line coaches, at Hitchin was reduced to 21 and the new garage provided six RTs for local services and four RFs for new route 716A. On 2nd November some of the short journeys on route 480 between Dartford and Horns Cross were extended off line of the main route to St James's Estate.

The Central Area had recently introduced express operation on certain routes where there was a higher proportion of longer distance passengers than was usual. This practice spread to the Country Area when an express service was introduced on route 403 on 14th December 1955 between Chelsham or Warlingham and West Croydon during Monday to Friday peak hours with buses running in service to Croydon during the morning peak and from Croydon during the evening peak. The buses ran empty against the peak flow. The Central Area practice of displaying white on blue destination blinds was followed. The buses only observed defined important stops and the operation was subject to a minimum fare of 4d and a slip board to that effect was displayed on the RTs. Certain journeys were withdrawn on the ordinary 403 route in consequence of this new operation.

Yet a further revision of fares took place on 18th December 1955, the implementation of which caused some problems for London Transport. Prior to 1953 all fares charged on the Executive's road services were authorised by the Transport Tribunal but with the passing of the Transport Act, 1953 that body's jurisdiction was restricted to the Special Area. Outside of the Special Area approval was required from the relevant traffic commissioner. The approval of the latter had not been obtained in time for this revision so only fares in the Special Area were increased. The 2d minimum fare was increased to 2½d and fares of 1s 1d and over were increased by 1d. Early Morning Single fares were now 7d, 8d, 10d, 11d, 1s 1d or 1s 2d according to the distance travelled. The reason for this second increase of fares within the year was that although London Transport had generated a revenue surplus of £5 million this was some £500,000 less than the figure required to fulfil its financial obligation to the BTC. It was not until 23rd September 1956 the increases for those fares outside the Special Area were implemented following the Traffic Commissioners' approval.

At summer weekends and bank holidays red buses were loaned to the Country Area to enable extra buses to operate. RTLs sometimes put in an appearance as shown by an immaculate RTL 800 which has been loaned to Staines and is being worked hard on route 441. *Alan B. Cross*

The introduction of new equipment at Aldenham Works in 1955 for producing destination blind labels led to a slightly revised style gradually appearing. In this view at Dorking Bus Station the bus on the left, RT 3812 on route 470, displays the older style label and RT 3148 on route 414 displays the revised style. The most obvious change was the front intermediate points blind which adopted four lines of place names instead of five. As the labels were often printed in advance and stored it could take some years for the change to work through all destination and route blinds. *London Transport Museum*

CHAPTER 5 DEVELOPMENTS 1956–1957

The number of vehicles required for Monday to Friday service peaked at 1,015 for the summer 1956 schedules. This figure was composed of 783 double-deck buses (RT and RLH), 168 large saloon single deckers (RF and 15T13) and 64 small saloons (GS). At the time of the production of the first allocation book for 7th July 1937 a total of 537 buses was required for Monday to Friday service. Apart from the few 15T13s, the Country Area now had a standardised fleet of just four main vehicle types, RT, RF, RLH and GS and proposals were being considered for new garages to meet the requirements of the new towns. A programme of conversion to one-man operation of the RF worked routes would also be introduced. The mechanisation of the ticketing system would be completed in this period but continually rising costs would result in further fares revisions. A new working week for operating staff would be introduced.

With the exceptions of Hatfield and Welwyn Garden City the new towns in the Country Area were all planned to have a bus station adjacent to the main shopping centre. A new bus station at Hemel Hempstead located in Waterhouse Street came in to use on 4th January 1956. Seven stopping points were provided for London Transport services and those of the independent operators B&B Services, Bream and Rover.

In consequence the following route alterations were made:

314A Bennetts End (Peascroft Road) – Hemel Hempstead (The Parade). Revised to terminate at Bus Station and certain journeys projected from Town Centre to Warners End (Martindale Road) via Warners End Road and Boxted Road. Also revised terminal working at Bennetts End, some journeys continue to operate via Leys Road in both directions to Peascroft Road, others form a loop working in both directions with no stand time via Leys Road, Howe Road, Bennetts End Road, Barnacres Road and Belswains Lane.

314B New works route Warners End (Martindale Road) – Hemel Hempstead (Maylands Avenue) as route 314A to Town Centre then via Adeyfield Road and Wood Lane. (RT)

334 Two Waters Garage – Hemel Hempstead (Maylands Avenue) via Durrants Hill Road, Barnacres Road and Bennetts End Road (works journeys). Certain journeys start from Hemel Hempstead (Bus Station) via Lawn Lane to Barnacres Road.

334A Two Waters Garage to High Street Green via Durrants Hill Road, Barnacres Road, Bennetts End Road, Longlands and Adeyfield Road (school journeys). Certain journeys start from Hemel Hempstead (Bus Station) via Lawn Lane to Barnacres Road.

804 New Sunday only limited-stop hospital route Hemel Hempstead (Chaulden) – Harefield Hospital via Northridge Way, Warners End Road, Town Centre, Two Waters, Watford, Bushey Arches, and Mount Vernon Hospital (set down only). Last pick-up point at Langleybury Church.

All services and journeys terminating at The Parade now terminated in the Bus Station although certain journeys were reinstated to The Parade on routes 314A and 322 on 2nd May 1956.

The following changes in Crawley New Town also applied from 4th January 1956:

405 West Croydon – Crawley (The Boulevard) with projections to Three Bridges and Goffs Park. One journey provided from Earlswood to Gatwick Road, Manor Royal.

426 Crawley – Charlwood – Horley – Crawley (circular). Works journey provided from Gatwick Airport Station to Pound Hill (Hillcrest Close) via North Road, Three Bridges and Worth Road.

426A Ifield (Bonnetts Lane) – Three Bridges. Revised at Ifield to terminate at The Parade via Warren Drive and Ifield Drive with odd journeys continuing to serve Bonnetts Lane. Certain journeys projected from Three Bridges to Pound Hill (Hillcrest Close) via Worth Road.

476A Langley Green – Three Bridges Station via Langley Drive, Manor Royal, Gatwick Road and North Road. Certain journeys now extended from Langley Green to Ifield (The Parade) and from Three Bridges to Pound Hill (Hillcrest Close) via Worth Road.

853 Three Bridges Station circular via North Road, Gatwick Road, Manor Royal, London Road and Three Bridges Road. Extended from Three Bridges to Pound Hill (Hillcrest Close) via Worth Road.

In addition to the above alterations one journey on route 438B was also projected to Pound Hill and certain journeys on route 476 were re-routed away from a section of Three Bridges Road to run via Mitchells Road and Gales Drive. On the same date certain journeys on route 447 were extended from Merstham (Delabole Road) to Pendell Camp. On 1st February Harlow local route 396B was revised to run from Potter Street to Fourth Avenue via London Road, Second Avenue, Howard Way and The Stow. Certain works journeys were projected from The Stow to Edinburgh Way and some journeys were re-routed at The Stow to run to Harlow (Post Office) via First Avenue. Stevenage local route 392A had odd journeys reinstated to Longmeadow on 7th March.

NEW LIMITED STOP BUS ROUTE 804

Hemel Hempstead and Northwood
(Mount Vernon Hospital)
and Harefield Hospital

Starting on
Sunday, January 8, 1956

LONDON TRANSPORT
55 Broadway, S.W.1. ABBey 1234

RT 1017 on route 314A to Bennetts End stands alongside RT 3611 on route 314 to St Albans in the new Hemel Hempstead Bus Station. Route 314 was replaced on 17th October 1956 by an extension of route 330. *Ron Wellings*

Events in the Country Area put tremendous pressure on available buses and crews with far removed garages often involved in contributing to the service. In this view RT 2512 on special route 406E heads a queue of eight RTs waiting to take the homeward crowds from Epson Racecourse. *B.A. Jenkins*

The driver climbs into the cab of RTL 743 working a special on route 410 from Bromley North Station to Biggin Hill air display. Note the paper bill neatly fixed in the blind box.

Ascot races always required much duplication on Green Line 701 and special service 443 from Staines. In this view at Staines Garage Cravens bodied RT 1472 in red livery, fitted with special blinds, lays over with RT reliefs for route 701.

The new towns posed problems with bus operation on account of the shortness of routes in the early days. One bus providing a 30-minute service on a route of, say, eight minutes duration would mean that the vehicle and crew were idle for 28 minutes in every hour. This was not conducive to efficient operation and as the towns developed a number of initiatives were introduced to make the operation more productive. Routes were linked across the town centre and loop terminal workings, with no or minimal stand time, such as on route 314A at Bennetts End, were introduced. Eventually some circular or even more complex routes appeared, so that minutes were saved by running buses empty against peak flows and interworking between routes became common practice. As the services built up more crews were required and in many instances staff from the Central Area volunteered to transfer to the Country Area. The new town development corporations allocated a quota of housing for such staff.

London Transport's road operating staff had worked a 44-hour week over six days since 12th November 1947. As a way to make the job more attractive to staff, the Executive proposed that 88 hours should be worked in a two-week period consisting of alternately five and six duties, thus giving staff one additional rest-day per fortnight. The revised duty schedules and rotas were introduced on a gradual basis during 1956. The standard working day of 7 hours 20 minutes plus a 40-minute meal relief was adjusted to 7 hours 38 minutes. In practice duties were of a variable duration and overtime payments were made in respect of duties exceeding the standard, subject to agreed limits. All duty rotas had to be adjusted to an even number of weeks and in some cases additional staff were required while in others the number of built-in spare duties was reduced to accommodate the additional rest-days. As a result of this change some Green Line coach duties entailed working a short spell of bus work at either the commencement or end of the duty. Due to this change in conditions the summer programme for 1956 was introduced in four parts with the first changes applying on 21st March:

309 Rickmansworth and Harefield (Truesdale Drive). Apart from one journey Harefield terminus curtailed to St Mary's Road.

310 Hertford (Sele Farm Estate, Police Cottages) – Enfield Town in consequence of the withdrawal of route 388A entire service to Sele Farm Estate including Sunday pm provided by route 310.

330 St Albans – Welwyn Garden City (Howlands). Certain Monday to Friday peak hour journeys introduced from Welwyn Garden City Station to Great Ganett via Cole Green Road. Also certain journeys from St Albans direction re-routed in New Hatfield to Green Lanes (Astwick Avenue) for school traffic.

340 Welwyn Garden City Station – New Barnet via Longcroft Green, New Hatfield and Barnet By-Pass. Service reduced to Monday to Friday

peak hours and Saturday early am due to introduction of route 340B.

340B New route Welwyn Garden City (Station) – New Barnet via Longcroft Green, Great North Road, Hatfield Town Centre, Cavendish Way, Bishops Rise and Barnet By-Pass. Supplementary service in Hatfield: Longmead (Cornerfield) and Hazel Grove South.

355 Borehamwood (Cowley Hill) – St Albans (Beech Road) via Radlett. Journey extended from Beech Road to Porters Wood and another journey re-routed to Marshalswick Estate.

388A Hertford (Bus Station) – Sele Farm Estate (Police Cottages) route withdrawn, service provided by 310 at all times.

803 New express route Uxbridge – Welwyn Garden City Station via route 351 to St Albans thence Hatfield Road to Fleetville and route 330. Ran Monday to Friday peak hours and Saturday except evenings. Monday to Friday between peaks service between Rickmansworth and St Albans. Level of service on route 351 reduced in consequence. The between peaks service from Rickmansworth to St Albans proved to be optimistic and was withdrawn on 17th October 1956. (RT)

852A Crawley Garage – Faygate Station positioning journey running direct via A264, route withdrawn.

On Good Friday 30th March an express version of route 457 between Uxbridge and Windsor was introduced with RT operation. The

It was standard practice to use a Green Line vehicle that would not be required for Green Line work until approximately 9am on bus work during the morning peak period. In some cases a bus crew was employed, in others a Green Line crew before taking up their coach work. RF 92 is seen heading for Ripley on route 415.
Alan B. Cross

In 1955/6 a number of express routes were introduced over sections of route where there was a higher than average number of longer distance passengers. The destination blinds were produced in blue and white as a distinguishing feature. Route 803 between Uxbridge and Welwyn Garden City was introduced on 21st March 1956. RT 4548 is seen in St Albans Road approaching North Watford, The Dome heading for St Albans. Note the blue minimum fare 6d slip board. The route only observed stops displaying a blue 803 Express E-plate.
M.G. Webber collection

There was always a heavy demand for point-to-point traffic between Uxbridge Station and Windsor Castle and on 30th March 1956 an express operation was introduced on route 457 at busy times. RT 3735 has been correctly turned out for the service. The slip board reads 'Non-stop minimum fare 1/5'.

The timetables advertised that connections could be made at Westerham between routes 410 and 403. This arrangement dated from East Surrey days when at one time a through route from Reigate to Sevenoaks was provided. RT 1032 heading for Sevenoaks on route 403 is seen waiting at Westerham.
G. Mead

nature of the traffic was such that only two fares were available, Uxbridge Station to Windsor Castle at 1s 5d and to Windsor Bus Station at 1s 6d. The main service was summer Sunday only commencing 15th July but a service was run over the Easter and Whitsun bank holidays and on August bank holiday Monday. The route was not shown in the staff timetables and buses were liable to be withdrawn if the weather was inclement. The combined rail-road tickets via Uxbridge to Windsor were available on the route.

The second part of the summer programme was introduced on 18th April 1956:

336 Watford (High Street Garage) – Chesham (Nashleigh Arms). Re-routed away from a section of Rickmansworth Road via Cassiobury Park Avenue, Swiss Avenue and Gade Avenue to serve Watford Met. Station.

346 Kingswood – Oxhey Estate (Heysham Drive). Certain journeys extended from Kingswood to Garston (Three Horseshoes) for school traffic.

346A Kingswood – Oxhey Estate (Hallows Crescent). Certain journeys extended from Kingswood to Garston (Three Horseshoes) for school traffic.

396B Potter Street – Fourth Avenue/Edinburgh Way/Harlow (Post Office) route withdrawn, see 805/A.

457B New route Slough (Crown) – Wexham Court Farm Estate via Wexham Road, Broadmark Road, Uxbridge Road, The Frith, Knolton Way and Wexham Road circular in this direction only. Projections to and from Windsor. (RT)

497A Clifton Marine Parade – Dover Road Schools (Gravesend lunch time works journeys), route withdrawn.

805 New route Potter Street – Little Parndon (Park Mead) or Northbrooks via Southern Way, Tillwicks Road, The Stow, Fourth Avenue thence Hamstel Road to Little Parndon or Haydens Road to Northbrooks. Projections from Potter Street to Epping Garage. (RT)

805A New works route Potter Street – Harlow Station via Southern Way, Tillwicks Road, The Stow, Edinburgh Way. Projections from Potter Street to Epping Garage and from Harlow (Post Office) via First Avenue. (RT)

806 New mainly works route Little Parndon (Park Mead) – Harlow Station via Hamstel Road, Fourth Avenue, The Stow and Edinburgh Way. Odd evening journeys from Northbrooks and odd journeys via First Avenue and London Road instead of Edinburgh Way. (RT)

The third part of the summer programme was introduced on 16th May 1956 when the following route alterations were made:

315 Woodside Estate – Purfleet Station (works journeys) route withdrawn, covered by routes 323 and 328A.

323 Grays – Orsett – Bulphan with one works journey from Orsett to Purfleet Station via West Thurrock. Revised from a daily service to a works service from Purfleet Station to Woodside Estate (Buxton Road) via West Thurrock, Grays and Rectory Road. Projections from Bulphan and Orsett in that direction only.

324	Belhus (Eskley Gardens) – Grays via Daiglen Drive, North Stifford and Nutberry Corner route withdrawn, replaced by route 328/A.
324A	Belhus (Eskley Gardens) – Woodside Estate (Buxton Road) via Daiglen Drive, Darenth Lane, Foyle Drive, North Stifford and Grays (Sunday only) route withdrawn, replaced by route 328.
328	Belhus (Humber Avenue) – Woodside Estate via Foyle Drive, North Stifford and Grays. Revised to run from Rainham (Monday to Saturday peak hours and odd journeys) or Aveley (Usk Road) – Bulphan via Belhus (Foyle Drive, Erriff Drive, Daiglen Drive), North Stifford, Grays, Woodside Estate and Orsett. The main service operated between Aveley (Usk Road) and Woodside Estate.
328A	New works route Purfleet Station – Woodside Estate with projections to Orsett and Bulphan via Stonehouse Corner and Aveley then as route 328. (RT)
328C	Belhus (Elan Road) – Rainham via Aveley High Street, Mill Road, Sandy Lane, and Wennington route withdrawn, covered by route 328.
332	Purfleet Station – Belhus (Eskley Gardens) works journeys route withdrawn covered by 328A.
332A	Aveley (Usk Road) – Belhus (Eskley Gardens) route withdrawn, covered by 328.
332B	Aveley (Usk Road) – Purfleet Station one journey only in this direction – route withdrawn.
403	Express journeys re-routed at South Croydon direct via St Peters Road.
406	Express service introduced between Kingston and Tattenham Corner Station Monday to Friday peak hours and Saturday except evenings with consequential reductions on route 406. (RT)
406A	New route Kingston – Tadworth (RT). Existing short workings on 406 re-routed between Tattenham Corner and Tadworth via Merland Rise.
449	Dorking (Bus Station) – Ewhurst via Chart Downs, Holmwood, Capel and Ockley. Extended from Dorking (Bus Station) to Goodwyns Farm Estate. One RT provided on Monday to Saturday for Goodwyns Farm Estate to Chart Downs Estate short workings. The timetable indicates GS workings.
464	Westerham – Holland via Crockham Hill with projections to Staffhurst Wood and Limpsfield and shorts from Oxted (Barrow Green Road) to Holland. Certain garage journeys between Oxted and Chelsham revised to double run via Tatsfield.

On 16th May 1956 route 328 gained a projection to Orsett formerly covered by route 323. RT 1088 is seen in the yard at Grays Garage equipped to work a journey to Orsett. The front intermediate points panel has been produced in the new style gradually being introduced which contained four instead of five lines of place names. The running number GY 220 indicates a duplicate and the 'to and from' slip board advertises Orsett Show.

The 16th May 1956 service revisions in the Grays area saw the withdrawal of route 328C running between Rainham and the eastern part of Aveley Estate (now renamed Belhus). RT 4194 stands at the Rainham terminus while working on the route. *Ron Wellings*

The Kingston to Tadworth shorts on route 406 were re-routed between Tattenham Corner and Tadworth to serve Merland Rise and renumbered 406A on 16th May 1956. RT 3730 is seen running under Kingston's trolleybus wires heading for Tadworth. Note the double depth slip board which advises of minimum fares that applied when proceeding from Kingston. *Alan B. Cross*

RT 3210 stands outside Staines Central Station (Staines Station today) on route 460 prior to working a journey to Slough via Datchet. Note the E9 stop flag with just two e-plates. At one time where e-plates were required this was the only size of flag that was used. *Alan B. Cross*

Route 424 which was worked by a mix of RF and RT from East Grinstead was converted entirely to RT except for the Crawley allocation of just one T. It should be noted that from the 5th October 1955 edition of the timetable, the eastern side of Aveley Estate was referred to as Belhus and the western side simply as Aveley. The withdrawal of the fragmented short routes in favour of routes 328 and 328A enabled three RTs to be saved at Grays on Monday to Friday. Despite this economy the allocation book for 16th May 1956 records the highest ever output for London Transport Country Buses on Monday to Friday of 1,015 buses formed of 783 double deckers (RT, RLH), 168 large saloon (RF and 15T13) and 64 small saloon (GS). By this time leisure traffic was in decline and the corresponding figures for Saturday and Sunday of 969 and 627 buses respectively do not represent peaks. The maximum ever Saturday output was 991 buses in the summers of 1952 and 1953 and the maximum Sunday output was 784 for the summer of 1952. Due to the Suez crisis there was no main summer programme for 1957 and no allocation book was published, so it has not proved possible to establish accurate figures for that period.

In order to attract more passengers to use the buses an experimental facility referred to as a 'Rover Ticket' was introduced for travel in the Southern Division on 20th May 1956. The tickets cost 5s 0d adult and 2s 6d child and were issued by conductors and one-man drivers after 9.30am on Monday to Saturday and any time on Sunday. They were not valid on sections of route where other operators' farescales applied (ie 402/3, 454/A Hildenborough to Tonbridge or 409 East Grinstead to Forest Row) or on special hospital routes 472, 483, 493 and 851. They were not initially valid on routes 335 and 353 from Windsor. From 1st July the facility was extended to the Northern Division with the exception of the self-contained Grays area. Other exceptions were 301 between Tring and Aylesbury, 359 between Little Missenden and Aylesbury and route 339 and hospital services 345 and 804. The original intention had been to issue Rover tickets only for the summer season but it was subsequently decided to continue their issue all year round. From 17th October they were not valid to Tilgate in Crawley or on newly introduced route 807. As a result of the introduction of Rover tickets the Sunday morning maximum cheap fare facility was withdrawn after the summer of 1956, but the rail-road tickets to Windsor continued. A series of leaflets to promote the facility titled 'Rural Rides with a Rover Ticket' featured suggested outings, a small map and a route description together with timings. For example leaflet number one offered 406 Redhill to Tadworth, 435 to Leatherhead, 408 to Merrow, 448 to Gomshall, 425 to Dorking and return to Redhill on 414. The term 'Green Rover' was used in publicity material following the introduction of 'Red Rovers' in the Central Area on 12th October 1957.

1

A TOUR IN SURREY

Rural Rides

BY LONDON TRANSPORT

LONDON TRANSPORT

ROVERS

ROVER TICKETS
ON COUNTRY BUSES
5/-
CHILDREN 2/6

Two items of publicity in connection with the introduction of the Rover ticket below.

N 8803

LONDON TRANSPORT
COUNTRY BUSES

5/-

ROVER DAY
TICKET

AVAILABLE
ON DAY OF
ISSUE ONLY

FOR CONDITIONS
SEE OVER

NOT TRANSFERABLE

RT 3121 sets down passengers at Windsor Castle having arrived from Uxbridge on route 457A which differed from the 457 by running via Upton Lea in Slough. The driver has set the destination blind ready for the return journey. *John Fozard*

In the major changes which applied on 11th July 1956 route 337 lost the lengthy Saturday projection from Hemel Hempstead to Watford via Sarratt. In this view taken earlier in 1956 crew operated RF 582 stops at Croxley Station while working from Dunstable to Watford. RT 3180 is seen in the background whilst working a Croxley to Garston short journey on route 351.
Ron Wellings

Following successful trials with one-man RF operation on routes 419 and 316, the decision was taken to convert a number of other routes commencing with the fourth part of the summer programme on 11th July 1956:

308 Hertford (Bus Station) – Cuffley converted from RF crew to RF OMO.

308A Hertford (Bus Station) – Little Berkhampsted converted from RF crew to RF OMO.

316 Chesham – Hemel Hempstead (Bus Station) converted from RF OMO to GS.

317 Watford (Leavesden Road) – Berkhamsted via Sarratt, Hemel Hempstead and Little Gaddesden. Withdrawn between Watford and Boxmoor Station. Certain journeys run from Two Waters Garage instead of Boxmoor Station and projections to Apsley Mills continue. Converted from 15T13 to RF OMO.

317A Hemel Hempstead (Bus Station) – Nettleden – Little Gaddesden. Revised to start at either Two Waters Garage or Boxmoor Station (via Fishery Road). Converted from 15T13 to RF OMO.

318 Abbots Langley (Hazelwood Lane) – Watford – Sarratt with projections to Chipperfield. Extended from Sarratt to Hemel Hempstead (Bus Station) via Boxmoor and Two Waters replacing parts of routes 317 and 337.

319 Chipperfield – Abbots Langley – Watford with projections from Sarratt to Chipperfield. Converted from RF crew to RF OMO.

319A Two Waters – Nash Mills – Kings Langley Station – Abbots Langley – Watford (works journeys). Converted from RF crew to RF OMO.

319B Two Waters – Kings Langley – Chipperfield – Sarratt (positioning journeys). Converted from RF crew to RF OMO.

319C Watford via Garston and Kings Langley Station (in that direction only) then Ovaltine Works – Apsley Mills – Hemel Hempstead (Bus Station) (works journeys). The Watford journey now terminates at Two Waters Garage and converted from RF crew to RF OMO.

319D Watford (Clarendon Corner) – Langleybury School via Garston and Abbots Langley (school journeys). Withdrawn between Watford and Garston Garage and converted from RF crew to RF OMO.

334A Two Waters Garage via Durrants Hill Road or Hemel Hempstead (Bus Station) via Lawn Lane to High Street Green via Barnacres Road, Bennetts End Road, Longlands and Adeyfield Road (school journeys). Certain journeys now extended from Two Waters Garage to Warners End (Martindale Road) via Fishery Road and Northridge Way.

337 Watford (Leavesden Road) via Sarratt (Saturday) or Hemel Hempstead (Bus Station) (except Saturday) – Dunstable. Revised to operate Boxmoor Station (via Fishery Road) or Two Waters Garage – Dunstable. Projections to Apsley Mills continue.

376 Luton – Kensworth with projection to Studham. One morning journey now provided from Whipsnade Zoo to Luton in that direction only.

376A Studham – Kensworth – Dunstable (AC Delco Works) (works journeys). Journeys provided between Whipsnade Zoo and Dunstable.

384 Hertford (Bus Station) – Letchworth via Dane End and Stevenage converted from RF crew to RF OMO.

384A Hertford (Bus Station) – Great Munden converted from RF crew to RF OMO.

384B Benington – Letchworth via Letchworth Gate (works journeys). Revised with a northbound journey Hertford (Fairfax Road) – Letchworth, southbound journey Letchworth – Stevenage (White Lion). Converted from RF crew to RF OMO.

385A New route North Watford (Douglas Avenue) – Holywell Estate (Tolpits Lane) via Watford Junction, Vicarage Road and Euston Avenue. (RT)

394 Great Missenden – Chartridge – Chesham – Hyde Heath – Hyde End converted from 15T13 to RF OMO.

394A Great Missenden – Chartridge – Chesham – Chesham Moor converted from 15T13 to RF OMO.

394B Great Missenden – Chartridge – Chesham (Nashleigh Arms) converted from 15T13 to RF OMO.

394C Amersham Garage – Hyde End (positioning journeys) converted from 15T13 to RF OMO.

394D Kings Ash – Chartridge – Chesham (Broadway) one journey projected to Hyde Heath and converted from 15T13 to RF OMO.

399 Hertford (Bus Station) – Coopersale Street with morning projection to Coopersale Common. Afternoon projection to Coopersale Common provided for schools traffic and converted from RF crew to RF OMO.

802 Stevenage (Hydean Way, Peartree Way) – Six Hills Way via Monks Wood and Bedwell circular via Bridge Road, Industrial Area and Monks Wood with projections to Hydean Way. Revised (i) intermediately re-routed at Monks Wood away from Elder Way and Great North Road to run via Six Hills Way direct; (ii) supplementary service introduced between Bedwell and Industrial Area via Bridge Road; (iii) Industrial Area terminus designated Six Hills Way (Gunnels Wood Road).

New Watford local route 385A was introduced on 11th July 1956 from North Watford, Douglas Avenue to Holywell Estate via Watford Junction and the town centre. RT 4722, fitted with a 'lazy' blind display, pulls away from Watford Junction bound for Holywell Estate. *Ron Wellings*

Amersham lost its 15T13 allocation on 11th July 1956 when the 394 group was converted to RF one-man operation. An immaculate T 780 is seen at Chesham working to Great Missenden on route 394. *John Herting collection*

Route 399 from Coopersale Street to Hertford was converted from RF crew to RF one-man operation on 11th July 1956. RF 685 working to St Margarets is seen in Epping High Street when new. *W.J. Haynes*

99

The mid-1950s represented the hey-day of Country Bus operation with just over 1,000 buses being required for Monday to Friday service. Leisure bus travel still proved to be popular at summer weekends and bank holidays as this picture taken on bank holiday Monday 1st August 1955 shows. Loaned red RT 2134 and green RT 3187 stand outside Windsor Garage before working in duplicate to Berkhamsted on route 353. *Alan B. Cross*

On the 319 group one working was covered by a GS from Garston Garage rather than an RF. Routes 308/A, 384/A and 399 had been worked jointly by Epping, Hertford and Hitchin garages since 1942 with buses and crews interworking between routes at Hertford. The Hitchin duties remained crew operated until 16th October 1957 when the allocation was withdrawn. The conversion of the 394 group to RF OMO saw a reduction in the need for the 15T13 class although one bus remained at Amersham to the end of June 1958 for use as a special duplicate.

Sir Brian Robertson, the Chairman of the British Transport Commission, gave a public undertaking that there would be no fares increases during the year 1956. London Transport was, however, faced with continuing increases in costs, particularly wages, and was authorised to impose a minor upward adjustment of certain fares from 2nd September 1956. The scale of fares authorised by the Transport Tribunal was as follows:

Up to 1 mile	2½d
Over 1 mile up to 2 miles	4d
Over 2 miles up to 3 miles	6d
Over 3 miles up to 4 miles	8d
Over 4 miles up to 5 miles	10d
Over 5 miles up to 6 miles	1s 0d

Fares for journeys over 6 miles also had minor increases. London Transport claimed that in many instances it was charging less and in some cases considerably less than the authorised scale and that it was not receiving the potential revenue to which it was entitled. In order to overcome this difficulty additional fare stages were inserted into fare tables, where necessary, and some 59 Country Area routes across the network were affected. Thus in some instances London Transport had achieved the situation that had been attempted in the March 1952 revision. The result of this adjustment was that some Early Morning Single fares and the cost of weekly tickets also increased. Conductors were urged to be vigilant in their fare collection duties to ensure that all fares were collected and that overriding was prevented. It was pointed out that one missed 2½d fare per duty would result in a loss of £5,000 per annum to Country Buses. Many passengers must have considered Sir Brian's undertaking to be worthless as a further fares revision was applied on routes or sections of routes operating outside the Special Area on 23rd September 1956. These increases which were subject to the approval of the relevant traffic commissioners had been deferred from the 18th December 1955 revision.

The winter programme for 1956 applied on 17th October when the following service changes were made:

301B Watford Junction – Berkhamsted via Watford By-Pass (works journeys). Revised to run between Watford Junction and Hemel Hempstead (Bus Station).

314 Fleetville – St Albans – Hemel Hempstead (Bus Station) withdrawn, covered by 330.

316 Chesham – Hemel Hempstead (Bus Station). Extended in Hemel Hempstead to Highfield (Bathurst Road) via High Street and Fletcher Way.

330 St Albans – Welwyn Garden City (Howlands) and Monday to Friday peak hour journeys Welwyn Garden City Station – Great Ganett via Cole Green Lane. Revised to run Hemel Hempstead (Bus Station) or St Albans Garage – Welwyn Garden City (Howlands) retaining peak hour journeys to Great Gannet, Hatfield (Manor Road), Hatfield (Green Lanes), Hatfield (Technical College) and Marshalswick Estate. Certain journeys also run via Apsley Mills.

353 Berkhamsted – Windsor. Late evening journey from Windsor revised to run to Chalfont Common.

354 Marshalswick – Fleetville – City Station – St Albans Garage and Fleetville – City Station – St Albans Garage – Marshalswick worked in two overlapping sections. Revised as genuine circular in both directions Marshalswick – Fleetville – City Station – St Albans Garage – Marshalswick. Terminus in Marshalswick changed from Homewood Road to Chestnut Drive.

355 Borehamwood (Cowley Hill) – St Albans (Beech Road) via Radlett. Extended from Beech Road to Firbank Road, projections to Porters Wood and Marshalswick retained.

368 Grays – Bata Shoe Factory via Chadwell Road (special journeys). Certain journeys run from Stifford Clays via Wood View Road instead of Grays.

388 Hertford – Tewin – Welwyn – Mardley Hill. Revised to run Sawbridgeworth – Hertford – Mardley Hill replacing route 389.

389 Hertford – Sawbridgeworth route withdrawn.

Hemel Hempstead bus services as shown in the public timetable book dated March 1957.

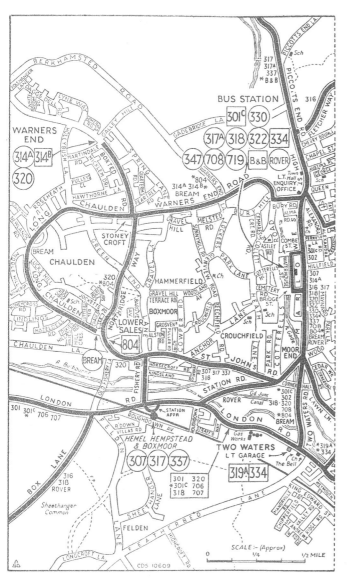

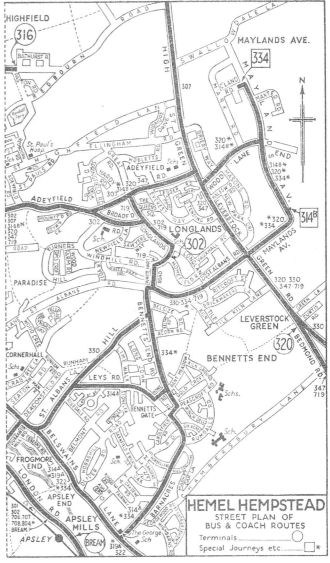

On 17th October 1956 GS operated route 388 from Mardley Hill to Hertford gained a lengthy extension to Sawbridgeworth which replaced route 389. In the off-peak period journeys terminated at Welwyn rather than Mardley Hill. In this view GS 44 waits in Prospect Place, Welwyn. *Pamlin Prints*

Crawley local route 476 was extended from Crawley Town Centre to Tilgate on 17th October 1956. RT 3501 with lazy blinds is seen working on the route. *Alan B. Cross/ Allen T. Smith*

Route 478 between Swanley and Wrotham was worked by an unusual mix of RT and GS types but the latter were withdrawn from 17th October 1956 when the service was considerably reduced and local fares were introduced between Farningham and Wrotham on Green Line route 703. GS 26 sets down a passenger while heading for Wrotham. *M.G. Webber*

405 West Croydon – Crawley (The Boulevard). One Mon to Fri morning peak journey projected to start from Tilgate (Canterbury Road).

406 Express service between Kingston and Tattenham Corner Station extended to Tadworth Station via Merland Rise and renumbered **406A** Express.

407A Windsor (Bus Station) – Slough (Trading Estate) via Chalvey (works journeys). Service reduced to one journey from Chalvey (Ragstone Road) to Trading Estate in that direction only.

426A Ifield (Parade) – Three Bridges Station with projections to Pound Hill (Hillcrest Drive). Extended from Three Bridges to Pound Hill (Grattons Drive) via Worth Park Avenue. Certain journeys to Hillcrest Close and Ifield (Bonnetts Lane) retained.

449 Supplementary RT worked service Chart Downs Estate – Goodwyns Farm Estate. Saturday afternoon service revised to Chart Downs Estate and South Holmwood.

476 Crawley (The Boulevard) – Langley Green with projection from Crawley to Three Bridges Station via Three Bridges Road or Gales Drive. Now extended from Crawley (The Boulevard) to Tilgate (Canterbury Avenue). Projections to Three Bridges retained and certain journeys projected from Langley Green to Ifield (Parade).

476B New works route Gatwick Road (Manor Royal) – Tilgate (Canterbury Road) via Southgate Avenue and Tilgate Way runs evening peak in that direction only, morning journey provided by 405. (RT)

807 New route Stevenage (Trinity Church) – Letchworth Station via Weston and Letchworth Gate with certain journeys running from Gunnels Wood Road via Fairview Road and Stevenage Station or Chequers Bridge Road. (GS)

In addition routes 323, 328 and 328A were re-routed in Grays to run via Southend Road instead of Rectory Road. In Stevenage routes 392A and 802 were extended further along Hydean Way to a new terminus at Wigram Way and at Longmeadow routes 392A and 801A were further extended along Oaks Cross to Longmeadow Shopping Centre. Additionally certain journeys on route 392A were re-routed away from Sish Lane direct to run via Haycroft Road and Greydells Road. Certain journeys on routes 476A and 853 terminating at Manor Royal were projected to a new terminus at Gatwick Road North (Rutherford Way). Route 313 was seasonally withdrawn to Whipsnade after 18th September and the express journeys on route 457 were withdrawn after 14th October. It is not recorded when route 474 to Burnham Beeches was withdrawn. Route 478 Swanley (St Mary's Estate) – Wrotham, which was worked by both RT and GS types, was considerably reduced being worked by RTs only, and local fares were introduced on Green Line route 703 between Farningham and Wrotham. On 28th November Littlebrook Manor Way journeys on route 477 were extended to Henderson Drive (Cavell Cres).

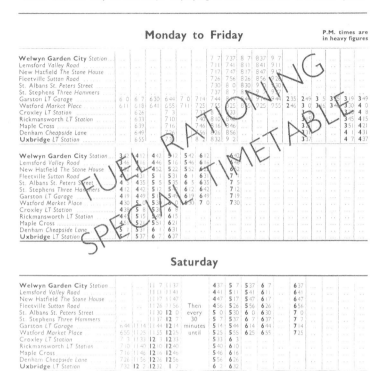

The year 1956 had seen many changes for Country Buses with massive service revisions and the introduction of the programme to convert most RF routes to one-man operation. A further factor was the ill-fated Suez crisis when due to the closure of the Canal, supplies of fuel oil became severely restricted. Fuel rationing was imposed from 17th December and while this resulted in an increased demand for bus travel, London Transport was required to cut its fuel consumption by five per cent. In the Country Area on routes with a 30-minute or more frequent headway, journeys were removed after 7pm on Monday to Friday, all day on Saturday and apart from essential works or hospital journeys all services were withdrawn before 1pm on Sunday. Reductions were also made to Green Line services and all excursions, tours and private hires were temporarily withdrawn. The result of fuel rationing was a six per cent increase in passengers across all London Transport road services and some augmentation of services was made during peak times. Twenty-nine additional RTs were licensed at ten Country Area garages.

On 23rd January 1957 in order to increase capacity over the Crawley to Horsham section single-deck routes 434 and 473 were curtailed at Crawley and RT worked route 405 was extended in their place. RT 2119 is seen heading for West Croydon. *Alan B. Cross/ Allen T. Smith*

Double-deck workings had been provided on route 434 between Crawley and Horsham and on the frequent shorts between Roffey Corner and Horsham. In this June 1956 view red RT 853 stands at Crawley, The George before working to Horsham. *Alan B. Cross/ Roy Hobbs*

As the crisis was gradually overcome supplies of fuel improved and Sunday morning services were restored to normal on 24th March and full services were restored on 1st April 1957 with some of the peak-hour extra services continuing. From 14th May fuel rationing for private motorists was abolished. The government imposed an increase of 1s 0d per gallon excise duty and there was also a price rise of 3d per gallon. This increased London Transport's fuel bill by 38 per cent and transport operators were given authority to increase their fares without the authority of the Transport Tribunal or traffic commissioners. On 1st January 1957 the minimum fare was increased from 2½d to 3d with certain exceptions in High Wycombe where the Thames Valley farescale was observed. The budget presented to Parliament in April contained provision for the repeal of the excise duty increase and operators were required to restore their fares to previous levels. Somewhat controversially London Transport was allowed to retain the 3d minimum pending the result of an application to the Transport Tribunal which had

already been made. Needless to say this action was not well received by the travelling public.

Some service revisions took place on 23rd January 1957:

307 Boxmoor Station – Harpenden (Masefield Road). Certain journeys re-routed to run via Lybury Lane Estate in Harpenden.

307A Apsley Mills – Harpenden (Masefield Road). Certain journeys re-routed to run via Lybury Lane Estate in Harpenden. The Harpenden terminal had been redesignated from Westfield Road to Masefield Road due to a change in the working on 11th July 1956.

396A Harlow Station – Hare Street via London Road and First Avenue, peak hour journeys via Edinburgh Way and Howard Way. Certain journeys re-routed away from Hare Street to run to Western Industrial Area (subsequently designated Pinnacles) via Fourth Avenue.

405 West Croydon – Crawley (The Boulevard) with projections to Three Bridges, Tilgate (Canterbury Road) and Goffs Park. Re-routed at Crawley High Street to run to Horsham replacing routes 434 and 473 over this section.

405A New route Roffey Corner – Horsham via Littlehaven with odd projections to Crawley Garage formerly 434A. (RT)

426A Ifield (Parade) – Pound Hill (Grattons Drive or Hillcrest Close). Extended to Ifield Station. Journeys from Bonnetts Lane and to Hazlewick School retained.

434 Edenbridge – Horsham via Crawley Down. Curtailed at Crawley (George), replaced by 405 between Crawley and Horsham. Re-routed between Ridleys Corner and Three Bridges Station to run via Worth Park Avenue. Projection from Manor Royal retained.

434A Roffey Corner – Horsham via Littlehaven with odd projections to Crawley Garage renumbered 405A.

457B Slough (Crown) – Wexham Court Farm Estate via Wexham Road, Broadmark Road, Uxbridge Road, The Frith, Knolton Way and Wexham Road circular in this direction only. Certain Monday to Friday peak hour journeys now extended to the Trading Estate via Bath Road.

473 Edenbridge – Horsham via Rowfant. Curtailed at Crawley (George), replaced by 405 between Crawley and Horsham. Projections to Manor Royal, Goffs Park and Blackwell County Primary School retained.

808 New hospital route Longmeadow – Hitchin (Lister Hospital) via Broadwater Crescent, Valley Way, Bedwell, Sish Lane, Stevenage and Little Wymondley. Sunday only conveying passengers to and from Lister Hospital. (RT)

Due to the Suez crisis fuel restrictions there was not a normal summer programme for 1957 but some minor revisions took place on 20th March. A journey on route 369 was projected to Marshalswick returning as route 313. A Sunday journey on Hemel Hempstead local route 320 was provided from Warners End to Boxmoor (St John's Church) via Northridge Way and St John's Road. Revised terminal arrangements in High Wycombe saw most journeys on routes 441 and 455 setting down passengers at the Guildhall and picking up at Frogmoor.

Further revisions took place on 1st May 1957:

306 New Barnet – Leavesden (Ganders Ash or Works) with projections from the Watford direction to Aldenham Works. Intermediately re-routed in Borehamwood away from a section of Elstree Way and Barnet By-Pass to run via Warwick Way, Chester Road, Balmoral Drive, Ashley Drive and Furzehill Road to serve new housing development.

396A Harlow Station – Hare Street or Western Industrial Area via London Road and First Avenue, peak hour journeys via Edinburgh Way and Howard Way. One journey now starts from Third Avenue (Todd Brook) running via Hare Street to line of route.

476A Ifield (The Parade) – Pound Hill (Hillcrest Close) works journeys. Journeys from Pound Hill to Gatwick Road (Rutherford Way) via North Road and Gatwick Road and a projection to Ifield Station introduced.

476B Gatwick Road (Manor Royal) – Tilgate (Canterbury Road) via Southgate Avenue and Tilgate Way works journey in this direction only. Journeys provided in both directions and projected to Gatwick Road (Rutherford Way).

498 Gravesend (Clock Tower) – Coldharbour Estate or Northfleet (Plough) via Dover Road. Through service to Northfleet re-routed to run via Painters Ash Estate and Springhead Road instead of via Dover Road direct from the Kent & Essex P.H.

Another addition to the Hemel Hempstead network was made on 11th May when Saturday only route 307B was introduced between the Bus Station and Chaulden (Lower Sales) via St Johns Road worked by one crew-operated RF.

A further revision of services took place on 12th June 1957 when the following alterations took place:

301C Dudswell or Berkhamsted Station – Hemel Hempstead (Bus Station) with projections to Maylands Avenue. Main service extended to Hemel Hempstead (St Paul's Road) via Highfield Lane.

316A New works route Highfield (Bathurst Road) – Apsley Mills via Town Centre and Two Waters. (RT)

319C Watford via Garston and Kings Langley Station (in that direction only) then Ovaltine Works – Apsley Mills – Hemel Hempstead (Bus Station) (works journeys). Revised to operate between Ovaltine Works and Two Waters Garage only.

324 New route Welwyn Garden City circular in both directions Knightsfield – Cherry Tree – Ludwick Way – Hollybush Lane – Howlands – Heronswood Road – Welwyn Garden City Station with certain journeys continuing to Knightsfield or on Sunday to Lemsford Lane. Replacing RT worked section of route 372A. (RT)

340 Welwyn Garden City Station – New Barnet via Longcroft Green, New Hatfield and Barnet By-Pass. Intermediately re-routed away from a section of Barnet By-Pass via Cornerfield and Birchwood Avenue.

344 Watford Met. Station – Aldenham Works via Whippendell Road, Pond Cross Roads, The Dome and Watford By-Pass (works journeys) certain positioning journeys run to and from Garston Garage. Re-routed away from Pond Cross Roads via Clarendon Road and Watford Junction.

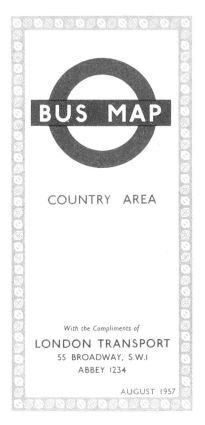

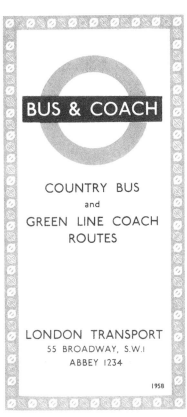

London Transport issued pocket maps for the Country Area from 1948. They contained a northern area map, four town plans, a list of routes and an index of places served on one side and similar information for the southern area on the reverse. Days of operation were indicated by different style and colour terminal boxes and symbols denoted where connections with other large operators could be made. Central Area routes which connected with the Country Area were also shown. Details of special works routes were omitted. From 1958 a completely revised map showing the entire network incorporated Country Bus and Green Line coach routes plus the Underground and main line railways. The reverse showed a list of routes, index of places served and a Central London Green Line map showing boarding points.

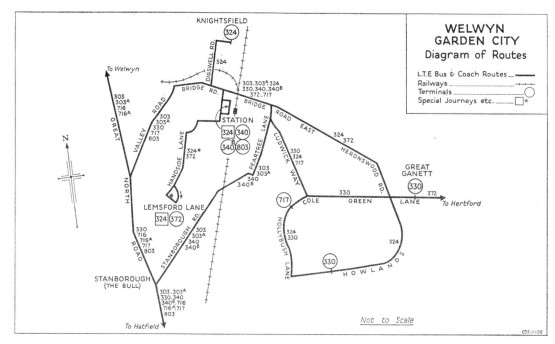

344A Watford (Met. Station) – Brockley Hill via
Whippendell Road, Watford Junction, The
Dome and Watford By-Pass (works journeys),
certain positioning journeys run to and from
Garston Garage. Revised to operate from
Tolpits Lane (Industrial Area) to Watford
By-Pass (Aldenham Road) with projections to
Aldenham Works.

344B Watford (Met. Station) – Whippendell Road
– Pond Cross Roads – The Dome – Aldenham
Road – Watford (Market Place) (works journey
in this direction only). Re-routed away from
Pond Cross Roads via Clarendon Road and
Watford Junction.

347 Hemel Hempstead (Bus Station) – Uxbridge.
Certain journeys re-routed away from a
section of Leverstock Green Road to run via
Wood Lane End and Maylands Avenue vice
route 347A. Certain Monday to Friday peak
hour journeys from the Watford direction
re-routed at North Watford to run to Watford
By-Pass (Aldenham Road).

347A Watford – Hemel Hempstead (Maylands
Avenue) route withdrawn.

358 Borehamwood – St Albans via Shenley and
Napsbury Gates. One morning journey
projected from St Albans Garage to
Marshalswick (Chestnut Drive) via Sandpit
Lane in that direction only.

372A Wewlyn Garden City (Lemsford Lane) – Great
Gannett via Ludwick Way and Cole Green
Lane. RT worked short journeys withdrawn
(see 324). RF journey from Welwyn Garden
City to Hertford retained for school traffic.

385A North Watford (Douglas Avenue) – Holywell
Estate (Tolpits Lane). Certain journeys
projected to Tolpits Lane (Industrial Area).

In Hemel Hempstead routes 314/A had a minor
terminal alteration at Warners End from
Martindale Road to Hollybush Lane. The
seasonal extension of route 313 to Whipsnade
commenced on 19th May and a Monday to Friday
service was added on 10th July with the last day

of operation on 13th October. For the first time
the extension did not operate on Saturdays.
Route 474 commenced on 14th July but the withdrawal date is unknown. The unadvertised
journeys on route 457 Express also operated.

On 2nd August 1957 a section of Brighton
Road south of Povey Cross was closed to facilitate the enlargement of Gatwick Airport. A new
road to the east rejoined the alignment of
Brighton Road at Lowfield Heath. Routes 405
and 851 were re-routed to use the new road and
the 438 group was re-routed between Tinsley
Green and Brighton Road via Gatwick Road
(north) and to double run via Gatwick Airport
(old) Station. The double run to the old station
was discontinued on or by 2nd April 1958.

A revision of fares took place on 15th
September 1957 when a new feature was a fare
for over one mile and up to 1½ miles. This
remained 4d but all remaining 4d bookings for
distances of over 1½ miles and up to two miles
were increased to 5d. In addition fares of 1s 5d
were increased by 1d, fares of between 1s 6d and
2s 8d were increased by 2d and fares of 2s 9d and
over were increased by 3d. The 7d and 8d Early
Morning Single fares were withdrawn and the
EMS fares were as follows: where the single fare
was 10d – 1s 8d the EMS fare was 9d, where the
single fare was 1s 9d or 1s 10d the EMS fare was
11d and where the single fare was 1s 11d – 3s 0d
the EMS fare was 1s 0d. The usual exceptions
were made where other operators' fare scales
applied and it should be noted that a number of
2d minimum ordinary fares continued to apply
in such cases. The inability of operators to
co-ordinate their fares increases caused a good
deal of additional administration as in this case,
just one week later, Maidstone & District fares
increased causing further adjustments to be
made on certain Country Bus routes.

As there had not been a major summer programme of route alterations due to the Suez crisis, a somewhat substantial winter programme applied on 16th October 1957:

301C Dudswell or Berkhamsted Station – Hemel Hempstead (St Paul's Road) with projections to Maylands Avenue. Saturday and Sunday journeys from Durrants Farm Estate at Berkhamsted now provided.

306A New route New Barnet – Leavesden (Ganders Ash or Works) as route 306 but running via Little Bushey instead of Bushey – Monday to Friday for school traffic. (RT)

307B Hemel Hempstead (Bus Station) – Chaulden (Lower Sales) via St John's Road. Garage journeys now work in service between Two Waters Garage and Chaulden via Boxmoor Station.

309 Rickmansworth and Harefield (St Mary's Road). Certain Wednesday and Sunday journeys re-routed at Harefield (Kings Arms) to run to Harefield Hospital.

321 Luton – Maple Cross. Former 351 journeys between Harpenden and Uxbridge renumbered 321 – route worked in two overlapping sections.

328C New experimental route Grays – Upminster Station via North Stifford, Belhus (Daiglen Drive, Erriff Drive, Foyle Drive), Aveley, Romford Road, Harwood Hall Lane and Corbets Tey. Monday to Saturday positioning journeys for route 370. Saturday late morning and afternoon service Aveley (Hall Road) – Upminster Station.

331 Hertford (Horns Mill) – Buntingford via West Mill or Braughing. Re-routed between Horns Mill and Hertford away from West Street to run via Pegs Lane to serve County Hall.

332 New route Amersham Garage – Quill Hall Estate via Stanley Hill positioning journeys for route 398. (GS)

Route 343 from Brookmans Park Station to Marshalswick was re-routed in St Albans to replace route 369 to Dunstable on 16th October 1957. RT 3621 is making the left turn from St Peters Street into Catherine Street in St Albans. *Alan B. Cross*

On 16th October 1957 route 301C had some journeys re-routed in Berkhamsted to terminate at Durrants Farm Estate on Saturday and Sunday. Roof box RT 966 stands in Hemel Hempstead Bus Station together with GS 80 on route 316. *Alan B. Cross/ Allen T. Smith*

| 334 | Two Waters Garage or Hemel Hempstead (Bus Station) – Hemel Hempstead (Maylands Avenue) via Durrants Hill Road, Barnacres Road and Bennetts End Road (works journeys). One journey now extended from Two Waters Garage to Boxmoor (Wharf Road) in that direction only. |

340A Potters Bar – Hatfield Garage (schools service). Intermediately re-routed in Hatfield via Roe Green Lane.

341 St Albans Garage – Hertford. Extended from St Albans Garage to Marshalswick Estate (Kings Hill Avenue) vice 343.

341A New route Marshalswick Estate (Kings Hill Avenue) – South Hatfield (Hazel Grove South) routed in Hatfield via Roe Green Lane, Meadow Dell and Bishops Rise. Saturday and Sunday only formerly short journeys to Hatfield Station on route 341. (RT)

343 St Albans (Marshalswick) – Brookmans Park Station. Withdrawn from Marshalswick and revised to run between Dunstable (Square) and Brookmans Park Station replacing route 369. Projections to Dunstable (AC Delco Works), Sandridge and Sandridgebury School.

346C New school route Garston Garage – North Watford (Maytree Crescent) via St Albans Road and Watford By-Pass. (RT)

348 Chesham Moor – Buckland Common or St Leonards. Intermediately re-routed in Chesham away from Great Hivings to run via Mount Nugent direct.

351 Harpenden (Kinsbourne Green) – Uxbridge existing route included in 321.

351 New route New Hatfield (The Hopfields) – Uxbridge via route 330 to St Albans and thence 321 with buses double running to St Albans Garage forecourt. Saturday afternoon only. (RT)

369 Sandridge – St Albans – Dunstable route withdrawn, replaced by 343.

381 Epping Garage – Toothill. Two Saturday morning journeys extended to Ongar Station.

389 New works route South Hatfield (Hazel Grove South) – Barnet By-Pass (Birchwood Avenue) via Bishops Rise, Meadow Dell and Roe Green Lane. (RT)

395A Hertford (Bus Station) – Ware (Fanham Common). Journeys from Fanham Common re-routed to Cross Street away from King George Road and Vicarage Road to run via Cromwell Road, Musley Lane and Garland Road.

396A Harlow Station – Hare Street or Western Industrial Area via London Road and First Avenue, peak hour journeys via Edinburgh Way and Howard Way. Journeys from Hare Street to Bishop's Stortford or Epping formerly run as 396 renumbered 396A and a regular service from Hare Street to Bishop's Stortford or Epping Station provided on Saturday and Sunday pm. Projection from Third Avenue (Todd Brook) retained.

398 Amersham Station – Beaconsfield via Coleshill with projection from Holtspur. Extended from Amersham Station to Quill Hall Estate.

398A Amersham Station – Winchmore Hill (school journeys). Extended from Amersham Station to Quill Hall Estate.

406C Earlswood – Redhill – Main Road – Reigate – Kingswood (works journeys). One pm journey extended from Earlswood to Reigate Garage via Meadvale.

424 Special works journeys Crawley – East Grinstead via Crawley Down or Snow Hill. School journeys provided from Crawley to East Grinstead (Blackwell County Primary School), all journeys now running via Crawley Down.

457 Windsor – Uxbridge via Uxbridge Road. Some journeys re-routed in Iver Heath between Five Points and Black Horse to run via Church Road and Bangors Road North.

457A Windsor – Uxbridge via Upton Lea. Some journeys re-routed in Iver Heath between Five Points and Black Horse to run via Church Road and Bangors Road North.

801 Stevenage Station – Shephall via Great North Road or Gunnels Wood Road (works journeys) route withdrawn.

801A Stevenage Station and Longmeadow via High Street, Great North Road, Shephall Lane and Broadwater Crescent (some journeys via Bridge Road, Fairview Road, Gunnels Wood Road and Six Hills Way back to Great North Road) and projections to and from Hitchin (St Mary's Square). Renumbered **801** and intermediately re-routed away from a section of Great North Road to run via Six Hills Way, Monks Wood Road and Broadhall Way. Regular Saturday service to Hitchin transferred to route 811.

804 Hemel Hempstead (Chaulden) – Harefield Hospital (Sunday only hospital service). Intermediately re-routed between Watford (Pond Cross Roads) and Shrubs Corner away from Bushey Arches and Mount Vernon Hospital to run via Rickmansworth Road, Croxley Green, Rickmansworth and route 309. Stops provided at Croxley LT Station and Rickmansworth. Converted from RT to RF OMO.

805 Potter Street – Little Parndon (Park Mead) or Northbrooks with projections from Potter Street to Epping Garage. Re-routed to Little Parndon away from Hamstel Road to run via Hodings Road with a clockwise loop working via Hobtoe Road to a new terminus at Canons Gate. Section to Northbrooks withdrawn.

806 Little Parndon (Park Mead) – Harlow Station via The Stow and Edinburgh Way. Odd evening journeys from Northbrooks and odd journeys via First Avenue and London Road instead of Edinburgh Way.
Section to Northbrooks withdrawn and revised to run to Little Parndon as route 805.
Journeys via First Avenue and London Road withdrawn.

811 New route Longmeadow – Hitchin (St Mary's Square) via Broadwater Crescent, Broadhall Way, Monks Wood Way, Six Hills Way, Great North Road and Stevenage (White Lion) Saturday except early am and evenings and odd journeys Tuesday afternoon. Buses run express between White Lion and Hitchin with no intermediate stops. One Tuesday journey from Hitchin runs via Fairview Road and Gunnels Wood Road. (RT)

854 New route Orpington (Kelvin Parade or Station) – Chelsfield Station circular in both directions via Spur Road, Orpington By-Pass, The Highway, Chelsfield Station, Warren Road, Sevenoaks Road. (RT)

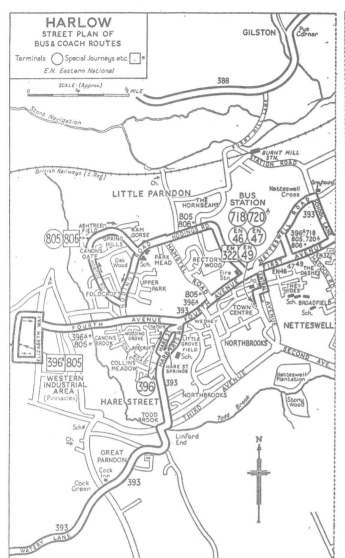

HARLOW
STREET PLAN OF BUS & COACH ROUTES

Terminals ◯ Special Journeys etc. ▢ *

E.N. Eastern National

SCALE (Approx.)

Harlow New Town services at December 1958.

When route 381 had been introduced between Epping and Toothill in 1950 the intention was that the route should continue to Ongar once the local authority had made certain road improvements. The extension finally came on 19th October 1957 when just two Saturday morning journeys were so extended. Traffic congestion would not be expected on a route such as the 381 but GS 37 has encountered a rural traffic delay! The lack of patronage is noteworthy and the extension was withdrawn in January 1958. *M.G. Webber Collection*

Route number 351 between Uxbridge and Harpenden was withdrawn on 16th October 1957 when all journeys were operated as 321. The change restored the situation that had applied prior to 12th November 1947. RT 4546 is seen at Rickmansworth Station heading for Harpenden despite showing a short working intermediate points blind.

Routes 307 and 307A lost the 15T13s a few months prior to being converted to RF one-man operation on 16th October 1957. Crew operated RF 646 sets down passengers in Hemel Hempstead while working to Boxmoor Station on route 307, despite the destination blind showing route 307A. *Ron Wellings*

When route 381 was introduced in 1950 it had been the intention that it should run beyond Toothill to Ongar but this was deferred at the time due to the poor state of the roads between Toothill and Stanford Rivers. The extension to Ongar attracted little business and it operated for just 14 Saturdays being withdrawn after 18th January 1958.

The following conversions to RF one-man operation were also made on 16th October 1957:

307/A from RF crew. The 15T13s had been replaced by RFs in July 1957.

333/B from GS – one bus saved; headway reductions.

337 from RF crew. The 15T13s had been replaced by RFs in July 1957.

342 from RF crew.

352 RF crew – Wednesday, Friday and Sunday service from Dagnall to Dunstable worked off route 337. The through Saturday service remains 15T13 worked from Tring.

364 from RF crew – Hitchin allocation only, Luton's remains RF crew.

390 from RF crew – Watton shorts remain RT.

393 from GS.

489/A from RF crew.

The following alterations in the South area were deferred until 30th October 1957 mainly due to strike action being taken at Leatherhead over the need to reverse without the supervision of a conductor at Boxhill:

Route 333 was readily associated with the GS type but from 16th October 1957 RFs took over the main route leaving just the odd workings to Chapmore End to continue with GS operation. GS 63 is seen at the Bengeo Parker Avenue terminus. Note the old style smaller bus stop flag which was sometimes used in the Country Area at one time.
Alan B. Cross

Further one-man operation of single-deck routes was also introduced on 16th October 1957. One of the routes concerned was 342 from Broxbourne to New Barnet – crew operated RF 574 is seen heading for New Barnet.
Remember When

416 Leatherhead Garage – Esher. Revised to run from Tadworth Station to Esher via Headley Court replacing route 435. Converted from RT to RF OMO.

422 Leatherhead Station – Boxhill via Headley with certain journeys running via Headley Court. Journeys projected from Leatherhead to Oxshott in both directions and one journey to Esher in that direction only and converted from RF crew to RF OMO.

426A Ifield Station – Pound Hill (Grattons Drive or Hillcrest Close). School journeys projected from Hillcrest Close to Worth School.

435 Leatherhead Station – Tadworth via Headley Court and hospital journeys Leatherhead – Leatherhead Court route withdrawn, covered by 416 and 462A.

462A New hospital route Leatherhead Garage or Station – Leatherhead Court. (RF OMO)

In addition the following conversions to RF OMO took place on this date:

304 from RF crew.
365 from RF crew – Luton worked shorts to Vauxhall Works and Batford Mill remain RF crew.
382 from RF crew.
426 from 15T13 – main service, RTs continue to be allocated to works journeys.
432 from RF crew.
434 ⎫ from RF crew – one bus reallocated daily from
473 ⎬ EG to CY. Crew operated RF retained at East Grinstead on Saturday and Sunday.

A joint operation with Thames Valley was undertaken in order to serve new housing in Britwell on the western edge of Slough. On 11th December the 484 group terminating at Farnham Road (George) had certain journeys extended to Britwell. The routes concerned were 484 from Langley Village, 484A from Datchet and 484B from Colnbrook. For a few weeks a temporary terminus was located at Monksfield Way (Doddsfield Road) with buses subsequently running to Doddsfield Road (Hawkshill Road). On 2nd April 1958 buses travelled further along Doddsfield Road to the junction with Kidderminster Road. Thames Valley's approach was rather simpler with route 64 running from Slough Station to Rokesbury Road, parting company from the 484 group at the junction of Readings Lane and Long Furlong Drive.

The service car miles for the year 1957 were 44.6 million (a drop of 3 per cent on the previous year), passenger journeys were 266.5 million (6.2 per cent down) and passenger miles were 705.1 million (3.5 per cent down). The decline in passenger journeys is particularly disappointing given the temporary increase in passengers due to the Suez crisis. The Monday to Friday requirement at the end of 1957 was 1,008 buses. Staff shortage was the continuing problem and as at 2nd July 1957 out of an establishment for 3,098 drivers and 2,929 conductors, there was a shortage of 94 drivers and 104 conductors across the fleet. The figures include Green Line coach staff. The events of 1958 would mean that the situation would be very different at the end of that year.

The one-man conversions of October 1957 resulted in a number of 15T13s becoming surplus to requirements. The largest allocation was at Grays where Rainham works route 375 needed four. In this view T 782 heads a line of the four parked at Grays Garage between the peaks. The buses worked in service to and from Rainham on route 371. In the background work on the garage enlargement which was completed in 1959 can be seen.

TIMETABLE

LONDON TRANSPORT

ROUTES 484·484 A·B

THAMES VALLEY

ROUTE 64

between

Slough and Britwell

WEEKDAYS

LONDON TRANSPORT

55 Broadway, S.W.1

Travel Enquiries — ABBey 1234

As passenger demand increased on route 396 due to the development of Harlow New Town, more journeys were re-routed to double-run via or terminate at Epping Station. RT 976 is seen working such a journey to Bishops Stortford. *Michael Rooum*

One 15T13 was retained at Crawley. In this view T 789 is seen at Horley working on the 424 supplementary service to Outwood. *Alan B. Cross/ Roy Hobbs*

In a joint initiative with Thames Valley, certain journeys on the 484 group were extended from Farnham Road to serve new housing at Britwell on 11th December 1957. In this view taken in May 1959, RT 4771 is seen in Slough heading a convoy of Thames Valley Bristols. This was one of the RTs which was placed into store as surplus to requirements and first entered service at Windsor on 14th May 1959. *Alan B. Cross*

CHAPTER 6 TROUBLED TIMES

RT 4787 stands at West Croydon before working the lengthy route 414 to Horsham. The gentleman seems interested in the E-plates, which contain the route destinations, on the bus stop flag. *Alan B. Cross*

The major event of 1958 was the seven week-long bus strike. In the immediate pre-war period London busmen were among the highest paid blue-collar workers but parity with other industries had been lost during and after the war as was evidenced by London Transport's continuing staff shortage. The introduction of the eleven-day working fortnight and a sick pay scheme in 1956, in addition to fringe payments for working at unsocial times, at weekends and bank holidays had failed to address the basic problem over pay. Staff found that they could earn the same or more in other industries without the need to work unsocial hours. The weekly wage rates for staff with two years' or more service at the time of the introduction of the eleven-day fortnight in 1956 were £8 17s 0d for Country bus drivers and £8 12s 0d for Country bus conductors. The Central Area equivalents were £9 6s 0d and £9 2s 0d respectively. These figures represent basic

rates of pay which, in practice, would be enhanced with payments by working unsocial hours, both scheduled and unscheduled overtime and rest-days. Immediately prior to the strike the trade union stated the average earnings of a Central Bus driver to be £11 5s 9d which compared unfavourably with the national average of £12 11s 7d.

In October 1957 the Transport & General Workers' Union submitted a claim for an additional 25 shillings per week in respect of all grades of staff that it solely represented – drivers and conductors and some engineering staff. The Chairman of the London Transport Executive was now Sir John Elliot who had replaced Lord Latham in 1953. In his earlier career Sir John had been a public relations man for the Southern Railway under the revered Sir Herbert Walker and had taken up his post with London Transport when the Railway Executive, of which he was chairman, was abolished in 1953. Sir Brian Robertson, Chairman of the British Transport Commission, opined at the time of Sir John's appointment to London Transport that he might become a second Ashfield. Such proved not to be the case. The T&GWU claim was rejected by the Executive on the grounds that it was both unjustified and unaffordable. After a meeting between both sides and the suggestion an inquiry be set up, the union requested that the matter be referred to arbitration in the Industrial Court and the London Transport Executive agreed. The matter was submitted to the Industrial Court in late February 1958 and a decision was announced on 11th March. In its expediency and wisdom the Industrial Court awarded eight shillings and six pence a week to Central Bus drivers and conductors and nothing to other staff. As might be expected this was unacceptable to the trade union which immediately asked London Transport that the award be extended to include all staff covered by the claim. Sir John felt strongly that having asked for arbitration the trade union should unconditionally accept the decision of the Industrial Court and became quite intransigent on this point. The trade union counteracted with a claim of 10 shillings and six pence per week for all staff covered by the claim.

On 2nd April the trade union gave notice to the London Transport Executive of an intention to withdraw labour on 4th May. Frank Cousins, the General Secretary of the T&GWU, saw Sir John the next day but the latter would not be moved. Allegations were now being made that Elliot was acting on orders of the Government. At the end of April London Transport agreed to include the double-deck Green Line drivers and conductors based at Grays and Romford London Road garages in the claim and to set up a review to look at methods of efficient working and to consider an award for single-deck coach staff. In what seemed to be a genuine attempt to avert strike action, the trade union claimed 6 shillings and 6 pence for all staff represented on the basis that it would not exceed the cost of the arbitration settlement; but Elliot remained firm. An appeal by Frank Cousins to the Minister of Labour, Iain Macleod, to intervene was unsuccessful and accordingly no London Transport road services operated on and from 5th May 1958.

At the end of May both sides were called to the Industrial Court and Sir John told Frank Cousins that he had nothing new to offer. The Prime Minister, Harold Macmillan, subsequently met with Frank Cousins and his senior officials. Macmillan suggested that the trade union accept the award of 8 shillings and six pence a week for Central Bus and double-deck coach staff and an amount to be negotiated for single-deck coach staff payable from the date of resumption of services. The pay of the so-called "excluded staff", which included Country Bus drivers and conductors, was to be the subject of a review

which would also include looking at economies in operation. The trade union representatives met the London Transport Executive and proposed that the "excluded staff" should be awarded 4 shillings and that the award should be back dated to 12th March, the day after the Industrial Court had announced its finding. The Executive rejected both of these points.

By mid-June it had become apparent that another round of wage negotiations covering railway and workshop staff was in the pipeline and it was made clear that Country Bus staff would be included in the process. The trade union delegates voted for a return to work and normal services resumed after seven weeks on Saturday 21st June. After further negotiations the "excluded staff" were awarded 5 shillings per week and single-deck coach drivers seven shillings and six pence.

There were no winners in this dispute. The staff had lost seven weeks' wages. Passengers had turned to other forms of transport, notably the private car, and the result would be a considerable fall in demand for bus travel leading to reductions in the level of service. London Transport's staffing position did not improve as there had been no recruitment during the strike period and in addition to normal retirements a considerable number of staff had resigned to take up other employment as they were unable to support their families without wages. The Times strongly criticised Sir John Elliot who was alleged to have mishandled the affair from start to finish. The relationship between London Transport's senior management and the T&GWU would be a difficult one for many years to come. Sir John Elliot was not invited to renew his position when his term as chairman expired in 1959 and became chairman of Thomas Cook. His place was taken by Mr. A.B.B. Valentine (later Sir Alec Valentine) who had joined the Underground group in 1928.

Staff at certain locations were concerned at the hardship caused to passengers visiting hospitals. On 5th May at Crawley a number of drivers and conductors offered lifts in their cars to regular passengers who used route 851 to Smallfield Hospital. Staff at Windsor wished to run Sunday journeys to Old Windsor Hospital but the union would not agree to such operation. Conductresses living in the hostel at Windsor expressed concern at having to pay £3 per week for board and lodging when they were only in receipt of strike pay of £2. A very few staff across the system refused to strike and continued to report for duty. This led to bad feeling after the resumption of working and there were instances of staff refusing to work with strike breakers. A recollection of a traveller on 21st June was that most buses had dirty roofs caused by standing under cover for the duration of the strike.

The year 1958 saw an agreement between London Transport and Southdown Motor Services over the working of routes in Crawley

New Town. Originally there was no difficulty with the boundary but the development of the new town had changed the situation. On 19th January route 483 (Crawley and Northgate) was withdrawn to be replaced by an extension of Southdown route 23 from Brighton and the introduction of a new 23A from Pease Pottage.

Following the major service revisions in October 1957, alterations over the next six months were few. Some minor variations occurred on 22nd January when certain short journeys on route 303 were extended in Hitchin from St Mary's Square to the Railway Station and school journeys were projected on route 336 from Chesham to Ashlyns School at Berkhamsted. On 5th February two school routes, 346D and 346E, were provided from Oxhey Estate, Hallowes Crescent and Heysham Drive respectively to Aldenham Road (Bushey Mill Lane) via Chalk Hill and Aldenham Road. On 5th March certain journeys on routes 314A, 314B and 334A terminating at Warners End were extended to Gadebridge (Howards Drive). Works route 377A (Markyate – Apsley Mills) gained a journey from Maylands Avenue (Cleveland Road) to Apsley Mills.

During the strike a handful of licences were granted to other operators, two of which were in the Country Area. Camden Coaches was authorised to run between Sevenoaks and Fort Halstead and Wright Brothers was authorised to run three routes to Harlow Station from Canons Gate, Hare Street and Potter Street. The summer programme was due to be introduced on 14th May; in the event the following changes applied upon resumption of working on 21st June:

301 Watford Junction – Aylesbury. Certain journeys from the Watford direction routed to Berkhamsted (Durrants Farm Estate).

301B Watford Junction and Hemel Hempstead (Bus Station). One journey revised to start from Durrants Farm Estate.

320 Leverstock Green – Warners End (Martindale Road). Withdrawn between Leverstock Green and Adeyfield (Vauxhall Road). Works journeys formerly running via Maylands Avenue and Wood Lane End revised to terminate at Maylands Avenue (Rotax). Sunday church journey to Boxmoor (St John's Church) retained.

328C Grays – Upminster Station via North Stifford, Belhus (Daiglen Drive, Erriff Drive, Foyle Drive), Aveley, Romford Road, Harwood Hall Lane and Corbets Tey experimental route withdrawn – actual last day of operation Saturday 3rd May.

337 Boxmoor Station (via Fishery Road) or Two Waters Garage – Dunstable. Certain summer Sunday journeys re-routed at Whipsnade Heath Cross Roads to double run to Whipsnade Zoo from 22nd June until 12th October. Passengers not conveyed between the zoo and Dunstable.

353 Berkhamsted – Windsor. Intermediately re-routed to run via Anne's Corner, Chesham Bois instead of Chesham Road direct.

362 Ley Hill – High Wycombe via Anne's Corner. Intermediately re-routed away from Anne's Corner to run via Chesham Road direct.

362A Ley Hill – High Wycombe route withdrawn, all journeys run as 362 – actual last day of operation Sunday 4th May.

362B Penn – Hazlemere – High Wycombe route withdrawn, covered by 363 – actual last day of operation Sunday 4th May.

363 High Wycombe – Totteridge. Revised to run between Penn and Totteridge via Hazlemere and High Wycombe. Early Monday to Friday journeys from Penn to Desborough Park Road (ex 362B) retained.

369 New route Aveley (Usk Road) – Ockendon Station via Foyle Drive, Darenth Avenue, Daiglen Drive, Arisdale Avenue and West Road. Monday to Friday peak hours and Saturday except early am and evening. (RT)

374 Grays – Uplands Estate – Aveley (Tunnel Garage) with projections to Rainham. Extended from Grays to Linford replacing route 380.

380 Grays – Linford route withdrawn – actual last day of operation Sunday 4th May.

394 Great Missenden – Chartridge – Chesham – Hyde Heath – Hyde End. Certain journeys intermediately re-routed between Lee Common and Chartridge to run via Swan Bottom.

394A Great Missenden – Chartridge – Chesham – Chesham Moor. Certain journeys intermediately re-routed between Lee Common and Chartridge to run via Swan Bottom.

394B Great Missenden – Chartridge – Chesham (Nashleigh Arms) renumbered **394** – actual last day of operation Saturday 3rd May.

394C Amersham Garage – Hyde End (positioning journeys) renumbered **394** – actual last day of operation Sunday 4th May.

394D Kings Ash – Chartridge – Chesham (Broadway) one journey projected to Hyde Heath. Route withdrawn, partially covered by re-routeing certain journeys on routes 394/A – actual last day of operation Saturday 3rd May.

400 New Sunday only hospital route New Addington (Parkway) – Warlingham Park Hospital. (GS).

406 Kingston – Redhill. One positioning journey from Leatherhead Garage re-routed to run via Ashtead Pond.

406A Kingston – Tadworth via Merland Rise. One journey projected to Reigate.

423A Watchgate (Hill Rise) – Joyce Green Hospital – Wells Factory. Watchgate terminus changed to Ladywood Road and journey from Longfield (Essex Road) provided.

464 Westerham or Oxted (Barrow Green Road) – Holland via Crockham Hill with projections to Staffhurst Wood and Limpsfield Common. Garage journeys between Oxted and Chelsham direct or via Tatsfield. Certain journeys now revised between Hurst Green Road and Holland to double run via Hurst Green Station and Pollards Oak Crescent.

465 Edenbridge – Holland with projections to Staffhurst Wood and Limpsfield Common. Garage journeys between Oxted and Chelsham. Certain journeys now revised between Hurst Green Road and Holland to double run via Hurst Green Station and Pollards Oak Crescent.

The ill-fated Sunday hospital route 400 between New Addington and Warlingham Park Hospital should have been introduced during the bus strike but actually started on 22nd June 1958. It failed to attract sufficient patronage and ran for the last time on 26th October. The driver of GS 3 relaxes during the lay-over period at the hospital. *Peter Jones collection*

Also planned to take place on 14th May 1958 was the extension of route 374 from Grays to Linford replacing route 380. RT 4177 is seen in Grays heading for Tunnel Garage in August 1958. *Alan B. Cross*

With the resumption of services after the bus strike routes 396A, 805 and 806 were re-routed to run via Harlow Bus Station. RT 1031 loads up for Potter Street whilst performing a journey on route 805. The tubular steel shelters were of a temporary nature and were subsequently replaced with modern structures more suitable for the new town environment. *Ron Wellings*

RT 638 is caught in traffic at Epsom Clock Tower whilst working a journey on route 406 from Leatherhead Garage to Kingston. The slip board advertises minimum fares out of Kingston. *Alan B. Cross*

RT 1035 stands on the forecourt of Chelsham Garage before working to Guildford on route 408. In the 1950s there was a proposal to completely rebuild the former East Surrey garage dating from 1925. The new garage with a capacity of 100 buses would have relieved pressure on Dorking, Dunton Green and Leatherhead.
Alan B. Cross/W.R. Legg

Rural services such as route 448 were supported by the more profitable routes in a form of cross-subsidisation. GS 25 is seen on route 448 heading for Guildford.
Alan B. Cross

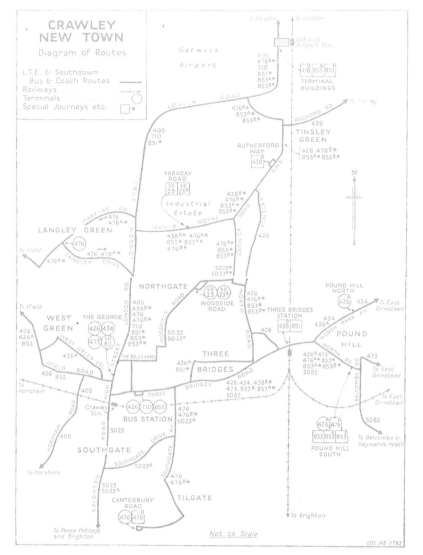

CRAWLEY
NEW TOWN

Diagram of Routes

L.T.E. & Southdown
Bus & Coach Routes ——
Railways ━┿━
Terminals ○
Special Journeys etc. ☐ *

Not to Scale

CDS JR5 11782

In 1958 one 15T13 remained at Crawley for use on works services. T 787 is seen in the garage yard with the blind set for route 853. *Michael Rooum*

Crawley Bus Station in Three Bridges Road was opened as planned on 28th May 1958 but was initially used by Southdown buses only. The following changes had been planned to commence on 28th May when in addition to the new bus station, a new Gatwick Airport Station was brought into use and applied from 21st June:

405	West Croydon – Horsham (Carfax) projections to Three Bridges, Tilgate (Canterbury Road) and Goffs Park. Re-routed in Crawley to run via Bus Station.
405A	Roffey Corner – Horsham via Littlehaven with odd projections to Crawley Garage. Crawley journeys re-routed to run via Bus Station.
424	Special journeys Crawley (George) – East Grinstead (Blackwell County Primary School) via Copthorne and Crawley Down. Terminus changed to Crawley (Bus Station).
426	Crawley (George) – Charlwood – Horley – Crawley (George) (circular). Revised to run Crawley (Bus Station) – Charlwood – Horley – Crawley (George).
426A	Ifield Station – Pound Hill (Grattons Drive or Hillcrest Close) school journeys projected from Hillcrest Close to Worth School. Re-routed via Bus Station.
438	Works journeys Crawley Down – Crawley (George) via Shipley Bridge, Tinsley Green and Brighton Road. Reinstated to start from East Grinstead running either via Crawley Down or Snow Hill and revised to terminate at Crawley (Bus Station).
438A	Works journeys East Grinstead (Bus Station) – Crawley (George) via Crawley Down, Copthorne, Ridleys Corner, Tinsley Green and Brighton Road. Revised to terminate at Crawley (Bus Station).
438B	Works route Crawley Down – Crawley (George) via Copthorne, Tinsley Green, Gatwick Airport Station and Manor Royal. Projection from Crawley to Pound Hill (Hillcrest Close) via Three Bridges provided. Now revised to operate Three Bridges Station – Crawley (Bus Station) – Gatwick Road (Rutherford Way).
438C	Works route East Grinstead – Crawley (George) via Snow Hill or Crawley Down thence Copthorne, Ridleys Corner, Tinsley Green and Manor Royal. Revised to terminate at Crawley (Bus Station).
476	Tilgate (Canterbury Avenue) – Langley Green odd journeys projected from Crawley to Three Bridges Station via Three Bridges Road or Gales Drive and from Langley Green to Ifield (Parade). Now re-routed to run via Bus Station and projected to Pound Hill (Hillcrest Close).
476B	Gatwick Road (Rutherford Way) – Tilgate (Canterbury Road). Journeys projected from Rutherford Way to Gatwick Airport (new) Station and new journeys from Rutherford Way to Pound Hill (Hillcrest Close) via Gatwick Road, North Road and Three Bridges.
851	Three Bridges Station – Smallfield Hospital. Re-routed to run via Crawley Bus Station.
852	Crawley Garage – Horsham via Faygate. Revised to terminate at or run via Crawley Bus Station. Projection to Three Bridges retained.
853	Pound Hill (Hillcrest Close) or Three Bridges Station circular via North Road, Gatwick Road, Manor Royal, London Road and Three Bridges Road. Re-routed to run via Crawley Bus Station.
853A	New works route Pound Hill (Hillcrest Close) – Gatwick Airport (new) Station via Three Bridges Road, Bus Station, Manor Royal and Gatwick Road. (Mainly RT)
853B	New works route Pound Hill (Hillcrest Close) – Gatwick Airport (new) Station via North Road and Gatwick Road. (Mainly RT)

RT 4765 was placed into service at Chelsham in March 1958 and is seen at Wallington on route 403B. Possibly following accident damage, two side panels have recently been replaced and no fleet name is carried on the offside. *Alan B. Cross*

Further one-man operation took place on 23rd July 1958 including Dunton Green worked routes 404 and 413/A. A curiosity on route 413 was a Sunday morning projection beyond Chipstead to allow passengers to attend the church service at Chevening. Crew-operated RF 653 stands at Sevenoaks Bus Station before working a journey to Chevening. *M.G. Webber*

The garage at Crawley built by East Surrey in 1929 was quite unsuited to the needs of the growing new town and the majority of buses were parked in the open. In this view RT 3717 stands in the foreground with RT 4755 and RT 3495 parked behind. *Alan B. Cross/ Allen T. Smith*

The seasonal extension of route 313 from St Albans to Whipsnade was due to take place on Sundays from 18th May and in the event took place on 22nd June. When the route had run at Easter on 6th and 7th April, Whipsnade buses had been re-routed away from St Albans High Street and Mayles Corner to run via Catherine Street and Folly Lane. The Monday to Friday service was re-introduced to Whipsnade on 23rd July until 16th September and from 18th September two evening peak hour journeys were projected to Markyate. These journeys were withdrawn together with the Sunday journeys to Whipsnade with the winter timetable of 15th October but morning journeys from Markyate were provided from December 1958.

Some service revisions applied on 23rd July 1958:

324 Welwyn Garden City circular. Sunday only journeys to Lemsford Lane withdrawn, provided by 372/393.

330A Welwyn Garden City works service Cole Green Lane – Black Fan Road route withdrawn.

340B Welwyn Garden City (Station) – New Barnet via Longcroft Green, Great North Road, Hatfield Town Centre, Cavendish Way, Bishops Rise and Barnet By-Pass plus supplementary service in Hatfield between Longmead (Cornerfield) and Hazel Grove South.
Extended on Saturday afternoon from Welwyn Garden City via route 303 to Hitchin (St Mary's Square). Reductions on route 303 short journeys to compensate.

342 New Barnet – Broxbourne Station via Hertford Heath, Hertford and Essendon with projections to Broxbourne Airport. Section between Hertford and Broxbourne withdrawn, covered by route 393.

372 Hertford – Welwyn Garden City (Lemsford Lane) via Heronswood Road. Extended from Hertford to Coopersale Street with projections to Coopersale Common in replacement of 399 and converted from RF crew to RF OMO.

372A Hertford – Welwyn Garden City (Lemsford Lane) school journeys via Cole Green Lane and Ludwick Way route withdrawn.

377 Boxmoor Station – Markyate (works journeys). Withdrawn between Friars Wash and Markyate.

377A Apsley Mills – Markyate (works journeys). Withdrawn between Friars Wash and Markyate.

384 Hertford (Bus Station) – Letchworth via Dane End and Stevenage. Projection to Hertford (Sele Farm Estate) provided.

389 South Hatfield (Hazel Grove South) – Barnet By-Pass (Birchwood Avenue) via Bishops Rise, Meadow Dell and Roe Green Lane. Revised to terminate at New Hatfield (Manor Road) instead of Birchwood Avenue.

393 Harlow (Green Man) – Hoddesdon (Middlefield Road). Extended to Welwyn Garden City (Lemsford Lane) via Hertford Heath and Hertford replacing a section of route 342. Re-routed to double run to Harlow Bus Station and a projection to Harlow Station.

399 Hertford – Coopersale Street with projections to Coopersale Common withdrawn, see 372.

407A Chalvey (Ragstone Road) – Trading Estate (in that direction only) route withdrawn.

441 Staines – High Wycombe or Hedgerley Village. Early am journey projected to Britwell (Kidderminster Road).

854A New route Chelsfield Station – Green Street Green school and positioning journeys. (RT)

The Hertford alterations saved one RF. In addition the following routes were converted from RF crew to RF OMO without major alteration – 404, 413/A, 427, 437, 456 and 462. On the 427/437/456 conversion the odd projections from Weybridge to Walton were withdrawn but projections to Weybridge (Lincoln Arms) were retained. In addition the projections on routes 344A and 385A to Tolpits Lane Industrial Area were curtailed at Holywell Estate.

Despite the move to increase a number of substandard fares on 2nd September 1956 London Transport maintained that a number of such bookings remained and a further revision of substandard fares on 59 routes took place on 10th August 1958.

Passenger demand had dropped as a result of the strike and London Transport decided that cuts would have to be made to services. In the Country Area ten per cent cuts were introduced with the Winter programme in October which resulted in 38 fewer double deckers and four fewer single deckers being required. The first Country Area casualty was Sunday only route 474 from Slough to Burnham Beeches which was not re-introduced. Revised timetables were introduced on 15th October 1958 and contained the following alterations:

304 Tyttenhanger – Whitwell with projections to Hitchin on Saturday pm and Sunday pm. Revised to operate St Albans City Station – Whitwell with projections to Hitchin retained. One school day journey and Saturday afternoon journeys start from Colney Street.

309 Rickmansworth – Harefield (St Mary's Road) with Wednesday and Sunday journeys to Harefield Hospital. Certain Monday to Friday journeys re-routed at Kings Arms to run to Harefield (Hill End) via Harefield Hospital.

314B Warners End (Hollybush Lane) or Gadebridge (Howard Drive) – Hemel Hempstead (Maylands Avenue). Intermediately re-routed away from Alexandra Road (direct) to run via Marlowes and Midland Road.

318B New school route Garston Garage – North Watford (Maytree Crescent) via St Albans Road and Watford By-Pass. Renumbered from 346C. (RT)

319A Two Waters – Nash Mills – Kings Langley Station – Abbots Langley – Watford (works journeys). Withdrawn between Abbots Langley and Watford.

320 Adeyfield (Vauxhall Road) or Maylands Avenue (Rotax) – Warners End (Martindale Road). Sunday morning church journey from Warners End to Boxmoor (St John's Church) transferred to route 378.

325A New route St Albans (Firbank Road) – Cottonmill Estate (Abbots Avenue) via Abbey Station and Maynards Drive. (RF crew)

Routes 427/437/456 were converted to one-man operation on 23rd July 1958. RF 671 is seen in Addlestone heading for Weybridge after the conversion. In this 1959 view the bus has been fitted with flashing indicators. *Alan B. Cross/Allen T. Smith*

Route 462 worked by Addlestone and Leatherhead was also converted to one-man operation on 23rd July 1958. RF 666 is seen in Addlestone heading for Chertsey. Note the 'Pay as you enter' transfer on the top of the nearside windscreen. *Alan B. Cross/Allen T. Smith*

The first casualty of the bus strike was Sunday only route 474 between Slough and Burnham Beeches which was not re-introduced for the summer season. RT 4107 is seen waiting for the next departure to Burnham Beeches. *LTPS/D.A. Jones*

On 15th October 1958 new route 385B was introduced to replace works routes 344 and 344A running via Watford By-Pass. RT 3191 is captured arriving at Aldenham Works prior to working an afternoon journey for home-going London Transport workers. *Ron Wellings*

335 Watford High Street Garage – Windsor. Afternoon school journey starts from Aldenham Road (Bushey Mill Lane).

336 Watford (High Street Garage) – Chesham (Nashleigh Arms). Intermediately re-routed to serve Chorleywood Station. Morning school journey projected to Aldenham Road (Bushey Mill Lane). Projections to Ashlyns School retained.

344 Watford Met. Station – Aldenham Works route withdrawn (see 385 group).

344A Holywell Estate – Aldenham Works route withdrawn (see 385 group).

344B Watford (Met. Station) – Whippendell Road – Watford Junction – The Dome – Aldenham Road – Watford (Market Place) route withdrawn (see 347A and 385 group).

346C Renumbered 318B.

347A New school route Watford (Parade) – Pond Cross Roads – The Dome – Aldenham Road – Bushey & Oxhey Station. (RT)

351 New Hatfield (The Hopfields) – Uxbridge, Saturday afternoon only route withdrawn. Actual last day of operation 11th October.

353 Berkhamsted – Windsor. Certain journeys projected from Berkhamsted to Dudswell for school traffic.

355 Borehamwood (Cowley Hill) – St Albans (Firbank Road) via Radlett. Extended from St Albans to Harpenden via Wheathampstead replacing a section of route 391 including journeys from Batford (Pickford Hill) to Harpenden. Certain short journeys between St Albans and Harpenden start from City Station. Section to Firbank Road and projections to Porters Wood transferred to route 391. Journey to Marshalswick retained. Converted from RF crew to RF OMO.

365 Tyttenhanger – Luton via Wheathampstead. Revised to start from St Albans City Station, projections to Tyttenhanger and Hill End covered by 391/A.

377B Apsley Mills – Cupid Green via St Albans Hill (works journeys). Extended to Friars Wash.

378 Warners End (Martindale Road) or Boxmoor (Wharf Road) – Apsley Mills works journeys. Sunday morning church journey from Warners End to Wharf Road transferred from route 320. This journey was converted from RT to RF OMO on 22nd February 1959.

385 Croxley Green (Manor Way) – Mill Way Estate via Vicarage Road and Watford Junction. Revised to run Croxley Green (Manor Way) or Holywell Estate (Tolpits Lane) or Watford (Met. Station) – Mill Way Estate with works journeys extended to Watford By-Pass (Savage & Parsons) and projections to Aldenham Works.

385A North Watford (Douglas Avenue) – Holywell Estate (Tolpits Lane) via Watford Junction, Vicarage Road. Revised to run Croxley Green (Manor Way) or Holywell Estate (Tolpits Lane) or Watford (Met. Station) – North Watford (Douglas Avenue).

385B New works route Croxley Green (Manor Way) or Holywell Estate (Tolpits Lane) or Watford (Met. Station) – Watford By-Pass (Savage & Parsons) and projections to Aldenham Works via North Watford Library and Watford By-Pass instead of Bushey Mill Lane. (RT)

386A Hertford – Standon or Buntingford positioning journeys via Wareside, Widford and West Mill route withdrawn. Positioning journeys for route 386 now run as 331.

391 Harpenden – Wheathampstead – St Albans – Hill End Hospital with projections to Hill End Station or Tyttenhanger. Main service revised to run from St Albans (Firbank Road) – Hill End Hospital with extension to Tyttenhanger. Projections and Saturday afternoon journeys to Sandridge, peak hour projections to Porters Wood and Hill End Station. RF crew operation retained, jointly worked with route 391A which remains unaltered.

396A Harlow Station – Hare Street or Pinnacles via London Road and First Avenue, peak hour journeys via Edinburgh Way and Howard Way and projections to Epping and Bishop's Stortford plus projection from Third Avenue (Todd Brook). Certain peak hour journeys now re-routed between Bus Station and Edinburgh Way to run via Fifth Avenue (as yet un-named), Burnt Mill Roundabout and western section of Edinburgh Way.

442 Slough – Farnham Royal via Stoke Poges route withdrawn.

444 Windsor or Slough Station – Manor Park or Whitby Road (Saturday only) route withdrawn. Actual last day of operation 11th October.

804 Hemel Hempstead (Chaulden) – Harefield Hospital route withdrawn, last day of operation 12th October 1958.

In addition the 319 group lost its GS working and route 331 was converted from RT to RF OMO but retained one RT on Monday to Saturday. Much of the 331 service to Horns Mill was withdrawn at this time. London Transport's share of joint route 359 was changed from one RLH to one RF OMO. Route 386 was changed from GS to RF OMO on Tuesday and Thursday, from RF crew to RF OMO on Saturday and was one of a number of routes to lose a Sunday service completely. Route 459 was converted from RF crew to GS but lost the GS in March 1959 in favour of an OMO RF. Route 466 which was allocated one RT and one RF had the RF converted to one-man operation.

Another bus strike casualty was route 331 between Hertford and Buntingford which lost all but one RT in favour of one-man operated RFs. RT 2674 stands at a dismal Hertford Bus Station before working to Buntingford via West Mill. *Alan B. Cross (D. Farebrother collection)*

Saturday only route 444 which supplemented route 446 was another casualty of the bus strike and ran for the last time on 11th October 1958. RT 3859 is seen opposite Windsor Castle whilst heading for Slough. *Ron Wellings*

Stevenage Bus Station opened on 15th October 1958 and was located in Danestrete. Modern shelters were provided and were no doubt needed at this stark windswept location. Eventually most routes would be re-routed to serve the Bus Station. *London Transport Museum*

Stevenage Bus Station was opened on 15th October 1958 with routes 303/A, 340B and 390 being re-routed away from a section of Great North Road to run via Six Hills Way and Danestrete, a new thoroughfare parallel to the Great North Road. Route 392 was re-routed away from Monks Wood to run via Six Hills Way and terminate at the Bus Station. Routes 392A and 808 were intermediately re-routed between Bedwell Crescent and White Lion away from Popple Way and Sish Lane to run via Cuttys Lane, Six Hills Way and Danestrete. Route 801 off-peak service and certain peak hour journeys, plus route 811 were re-routed at Six Hills Way to run via the Bus Station. Certain works journeys on route 802 terminating at Gunnels Wood Road were projected to the Bus Station. Those journeys terminating on route 807 at Stevenage (Trinity Church) were projected to the Bus Station. In addition certain journeys on routes 303B, 801 and 802 were revised to terminate at Gunnels Wood Road (South).

The second phase of the winter programme applied to the South and South-East districts and came into effect on 29th October 1958:

400 New Addington (Parkway) – Warlingham Park Hospital route withdrawn, last day of operation Sunday 26th October 1958.

415 Guildford – Ripley – Ockham. Withdrawn between Ripley and Ockham.

416 Tadworth Station to Esher via Headley Court. Revised on Sunday to run from Boxhill to Esher covering loss of Sunday service on route 422.

423 Longfield – Crockenhill via Dartford and Birchwood. Withdrawn between Swanley and Crockenhill and revised to terminate at Swanley Garage.

424 Reigate Station – East Grinstead (Stone Quarry Estate), with supplementary services to Horne and Outwood and special journeys between Crawley and East Grinstead. Sections to Horne and Outwood withdrawn.

425 Dorking North Station – Guildford. Journey from Peaslake to Guildford provided (in that direction only) from Monday 3rd November.

449 Dorking (Bus Station) – Ewhurst (GS) and supplementary service Goodwyns Farm Estate – Chart Downs Estate or South Holmwood (RT). Main route to Ewhurst withdrawn. Some Monday to Friday GS workings retained and GS on Sunday.

467A Dartford (Bow Arrow Lane) – Wilmington or Horton Kirby (Sunday pm only) route withdrawn.

468 Chessington Zoo – Epsom – Leatherhead with projections to Effingham. Projections to Effingham withdrawn.

470 Dorking – Warlingham with projections to Chelsham. Extended from Warlingham to Warlingham Park Hospital or Farleigh with corresponding reductions on routes 403A and 403B to achieve headway reductions on common section between Wallington and Warlingham.

479 Farningham – Dartford via Horton Kirby and Darenth route withdrawn.

492 Gravesend – West Kingsdown via Southfleet and Westwood route withdrawn.

854 Orpington (Kelvin Parade or Station) – Chelsfield Station circular in both directions revised to operate Chelsfield Station – Sevenoaks Road – Orpington Station – Ramsden Estate (Petton Grove). Certain journeys continue to run via Orpington By-Pass and projection to Green Street Green.

Top: Further cuts after the bus strike came into effect in the South and South East Districts on 29th October 1958. Route 449 lost its GS operated lengthy rural projection to Ewhurst becoming merely a Dorking local route, albeit retaining some GS worked journeys. In this view RT 3515 calls at Dorking Bus Station whilst working on the local route. The bus shows signs of tree damage on the front dome. *Alan B. Cross/Allen T. Smith*

Centre: Route 479 from Farningham to Dartford via Darenth had been introduced in 1949 as one of a number of rural routes with a section serving areas that had not previously been on a bus route. It was withdrawn in October 1958 following a review of passenger usage of such routes in the wake of the bus strike. The loss of the route meant an end of GSs at Swanley Garage.

Right: On 29th October 1958 route 854 was revised to operate between Chelsfield Station and Orpington, Ramsden Estate. RT 2258 is seen at Orpington Station bound for Ramsden Estate. *Alan B. Cross*

In addition routes 412 and 425 were converted from RF crew to RF OMO and route 428 lost its RTs in favour of OMO RFs. One GS working on 451/490 was replaced by one RF OMO. Somewhat strangely a GS working was allocated to RT operated route 453 from Chelsham.

As can be seen the effect of the strike with the consequential drop in passenger demand was far reaching with a number of rural routes being completely withdrawn. The biggest loss was in leisure travel and headway reductions were made on a number of routes especially in the evenings and at weekends. In addition the Sunday service was completely withdrawn on 13 routes although in a few cases it was reinstated for the summer. This pattern of service reductions was to become normal for years to come. In the case of the withdrawn sections of route 424 to Horne and Outwood an independent operator, Browne's Transport (Redhill), was granted consent by London Transport to provide an alternative service which it did from 7th March 1959.

On 10th December 1958 route 481 was converted from GS to RF OMO. The first inroads into the GS class took place with the Monday to Friday requirement being 57 buses, eight fewer than before the strike.

A minor alteration took place on 7th January 1959 when a journey on route 476A was projected from Rutherford Way to Gatwick Airport Station.

On 21st January a route 334A journey was extended from High Street Green to Maylands Avenue (Rotax); route 377B was intermediately re-routed between Belswains Lane and Cupid Green to run via Leys Road, Bennetts End Road, St Albans Road, Maylands Avenue and Swallowdale Lane; and certain journeys on routes 370/A were projected to Brentwood Road Estate at Chadwell St Mary. On 4th February certain journeys on route 335 were re-routed to serve Leachcroft Estate on the north side of Gold Hill Common. In Stevenage on 17th February certain journeys on route 801 were extended from Longmeadow to Girls' Grammar School.

New garages were built at both Hatfield and Stevenage based on the Garston principle of a separate administration block but were rather more modest establishments. The administration and canteen blocks were single storey and the running shed could accommodate 49 buses. The garages were equipped to perform routine main-tenance only with buses going to parent sheds for heavier maintenance. The new garage at Hatfield was located on the north side of St Albans Road virtually opposite the old premises which dated from 1922. It was opened on 18th February 1959 and no alterations were made to existing services at the time.

The old garage at Hatfield opened by National in 1922 was replaced by new premises virtually opposite on 18th February 1959. In this view taken in 1955 RT 1095 stands in the entrance. A good range of panel timetables and other London Transport publicity material is displayed on the frontage. *London Transport Museum*

A general view of the new Hatfield Garage with the enquiry office, administration and canteen block on the right and the running shed in the background. Open parking was available for buses on either side of the running shed. *London Transport Museum*

The new garage at Stevenage located on the west side of Danestrete opened on 29th April 1959 and replaced Hitchin Garage and the temporary shed in Fishers Green Road, Stevenage. The administration block frontage incorporates an enquiry office and canteen and a through road is provided between this block and the running shed.
London Transport Museum

The new premises in Stevenage were located on the west side of Danestrete a little to the south of the Bus Station and opened on 29th April 1959. The temporary shed in Fishers Green Road and Hitchin Garage were both closed and the following route alterations were made in the North Area at this time:

303B   Hitchin Station – Gunnels Wood Road (South) via Broomin Green route withdrawn, see 801A.

343A   New route Studham or Whipsnade Zoo – Kensworth – Dunstable (AC Delco Works) (RF OMO) – route 376A renumbered.

356   Luton – Flamstead route withdrawn covered by extension of 364.

364   Luton – Hitchin. Revised to operate from Flamstead to Hitchin. (RF OMO)

364A   New route Kensworth – Hitchin with works projections to Studham and Whipsnade Zoo. Extended from Kensworth to Whipsnade Zoo on summer Sunday afternoons. (RF OMO)

376   Luton – Flamstead with projections to Studham and Whipsnade Zoo. Route withdrawn covered by new route 364A.

376A   Studham or Whipsnade Zoo – Kensworth – Dunstable (AC Delco Works) renumbered **343A** and converted from RT to RF OMO.

392   Stevenage Station – Stevenage (Bus Station) via Haycroft Road, Popple Way, Bedwell Crescent, Cuttys Lane and Six Hills Way. One journey projected from Six Hills Way to Gunnels Wood Road (South).

392A   Hitchin (St Mary's Square) or Stevenage Station – Hydean Way (Peartree Way) via Bus Station, Six Hills Way, Cuttys Lane, Bedwell Crescent, Colestrete and Valley Way. Extended from Hydean Way to Bandley Hill and one journey re-routed to Longmeadow.

801   Hitchin (St Mary's Square) or Stevenage Station – Longmeadow via Bus Station, Monks Wood Way and Broadhall Way and Broadwater Crescent with certain journeys projected to Girls' Grammar School. Also peak hour journeys via Bridge Road, Fairview Road, Gunnels Wood Road and Six Hills Way. Now revised with certain journeys extended to Hitchin Station.

801A   New works route Hitchin Station – Longmeadow via Stevenage Station, Fairview Road, Gunnels Wood Road, Six Hills Way, Monks Wood Way and Broadhall Way and Broadwater Crescent.

802   Hydean Way (Wigram Way) works circular via Bedwell Crescent, Popple Way, Sish Lane, Bridge Road, Gunnels Wood Road, Six Hills Way or Monks Wood, Bedwell Crescent. Extended from Hydean Way to Bandley Hill.

807   Stevenage (Bus Station) – Letchworth Station via Weston and Letchworth Gate with certain journeys running from Gunnels Wood Road via Fairview Road and Stevenage Station or Chequers Bridge Road. Certain journeys terminating at Gunnels Wood Road now extended to the Bus Station.

811   Longmeadow – Hitchin (St Mary's Square) express between Stevenage and Hitchin. Saturday service withdrawn, covered by 801 leaving only Tuesday service. One journey starts from Girls' Grammar School.

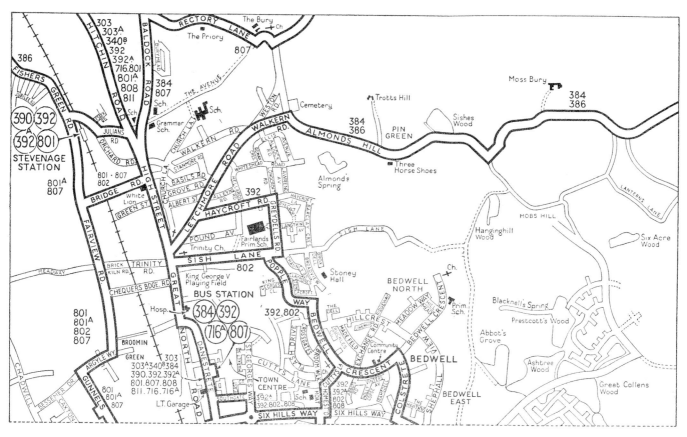

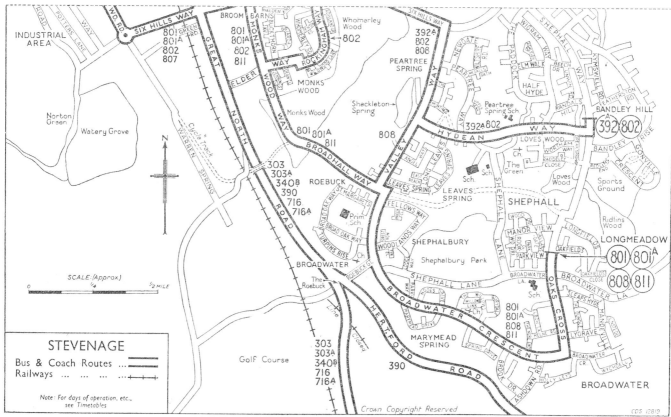

Stevenage bus services at the time the town's bus station opened, 15th October 1958.

With the new town routes becoming ever more complex and subject to frequent changes the practice of providing detailed intermediate point blinds was discontinued and in the case of Stevenage most workings could be covered by displaying 'New Town Service'. RT 3614 is seen in Stevenage High Street heading for the railway station on route 392A. *Ron Wellings*

Routes 392/A, 801, 808 and 811 were intermediately re-routed away from a section of Six Hills Way via St Georges Way and Southgate. Working in the Industrial Area was simplified with all journeys running via Gunnels Wood Road with Caxton Way becoming unserved. Route 364 was converted from a mix of RF crew and OMO working to full OMO with the Hitchin allocation being transferred to Luton. The works journeys on 365 were also converted from RF crew to one-man operation.

The extension of 364 and the new 364A enabled the sections from Luton to Flamstead and Kensworth and the Dunstable works journeys to be converted from RT to RF OMO. Stevenage Garage just provided supplementary journeys on the 364 from Hitchin to Preston, some of which remained crew operated.

GS 2 demonstrates the need for small buses on rural routes as it passes a motor car in a narrow lane whilst working from Stevenage to Letchworth on route 807. *Ron Wellings*

RT 1073 passes through a busy Watford High Street heading for the revised terminus of Leavesden Road introduced for routes 335 and 336 when Watford High Street Garage closed on 29th April 1959. A group of blind musicians busk at the kerbside. *Alan B. Cross/ Allen T. Smith*

Ever since Garston Garage, with its capacity for 150 buses, had opened in 1952, various proposals were put forward that Watford High Street Garage should be closed. Between 1954 and 1958 Garston had been used to store brand new unwanted buses and with the reduction in requirements after the strike, the position was reviewed and the decision was made to close Watford High Street Garage and with effect from 29th April 1959 all operations were transferred to Garston and the following changes made:

335 Watford (High Street Garage) – Windsor. Changed to terminate at Leavesden Road with projections to Garston Garage. Afternoon school journey from Aldenham Road (Bushey Mill Lane) transferred to route 336.

336 Watford (High Street Garage) – Chesham (Nashleigh Arms) with a morning school journey projected to Aldenham Road (Bushey Mill Lane). Watford terminus changed to Leavesden Road and afternoon school journey provided from Bushey Hall Hotel. Projection to Ashlyns School retained.

345 Watford (High Street Garage) – Napsbury Hospital. Revised to start from Bushey & Oxhey Station.

385A Croxley Green (Manor Way) or Holywell Estate (Tolpits Lane) or Watford (Met. Station) – North Watford (Douglas Avenue). Extended from Douglas Avenue to Garston Garage via Meriden Estate.

The opportunity was taken at this time to rationalise the routeings of the Vicarage Road services in West Watford. Buses to Holywell Estate proceeded from Queen's Avenue via Hagden Lane instead of Euston Avenue, buses to Watford Met. Station ran from Queen's Avenue via Hagden Lane to Station Approach instead of a short section of Whippendell Road and buses to Croxley Green ran via Queen's Avenue and Whippendell Road with the exception of two Sunday journeys which ran via Hagden Lane for passengers visiting Holywell Hospital.

Journeys to and from Garston Garage via Watford Junction and St Albans Road were provided on routes 306, 311 and 312 and via Pond Cross Roads and St Albans Road on routes 346 and 346A. Thus with the Monday to Friday requirement at Garston increased from 67 to 112 buses, the garage was finally working at something like its intended capacity. Within months after the closure of Watford High Street Garage management produced a report about the lack of suitable relief points in Watford – something which might reasonably have been considered beforehand. Crews on routes 306 and 311 usually took their meal relief in the Temperance Tea Rooms at Watford Junction while crew changes on route 385 took place at St Albans Road, Bushey Mill Lane. From 25th May 1960 certain journeys on routes 346 and 346A were projected from Kingswood to Garston Garage via Sheepcot Lane for crew purposes.

The first part of the summer programme came into operation on 13th May 1959 when the following route alterations took place:

323 Purfleet Station – Woodside Estate (Buxton Road) via West Thurrock, Grays and Rectory Road and projections from Bulphan (in that direction only). Bulphan projections withdrawn, see 399.

328 Rainham (Monday to Saturday peak hours and odd journeys) or Aveley (Usk Road) – Bulphan. Main service withdrawn east of Woodside Estate with certain projections to Orsett, see 399.

328A Purfleet Station – Woodside Estate with projections to Orsett and Bulphan. Service east of Woodside Estate withdrawn with the exception of one journey on Thursday only from Orsett to Purfleet, see 399.

348 Chesham Moor – Buckland Common or St Leonards. Journeys to and from Amersham Garage provided.

348A Chesham Moor or Chesham Broadway – Pond Park Estate. Journeys to and from Amersham Garage provided.

374 Linford – Grays – Uplands Estate – Aveley (Tunnel Garage) with projections to Rainham. Converted from RT to RF OMO.

375 Rainham Ferry – Rainham with projections to White Post Corner (works journeys). Projections to White Post Corner withdrawn and converted from 15T13 to RF OMO.

397 Chesham Moor or Chesham Broadway – Tring. Journeys to and from Amersham Garage provided.

GS 61 is seen in Chesham working on local route 348A to and from Pond Park Estate. *Bus of Yesteryear*

The requirement for four 15T13s at Grays came to an end on 13th May 1959 when route 375 was involved in what turned out to be a disastrous conversion to RF one-man operation. After the conversion the short works route lasted only a matter of weeks. T 795 is seen working the service. *Michael Rooum*

Routes 374 and 399 were converted from RT to RF one-man operation on 13th May 1959 but the loss of route 375 apparently caused problems with the scheme. The routes were converted to RT operation on 14th October 1959. RF 578 on route 399 sits alongside Green Line RT 4502 on Grays Garage forecourt.

399	New route Bulphan – Aveley (Tunnel Garage) with projections to Rainham via Orsett, Southend Road, Grays, West Thurrock, Stonehouse Lane and Uplands Estate. RF OMO
440	Redhill – Salfords. Revised to run from Woldingham to Salfords with certain journeys projected from Redhill to Reigate Garage both via Blackborough Road and via Earlswood and Meadvale. Converted from RF crew to RF OMO.
440A	Redhill – Redstone Estate. Revised to run from Woldingham to Redstone Estate with certain journeys projected from Redhill to Reigate Garage via Blackborough Road. Converted from RF crew to RF OMO.
441A	New Sunday only route Windsor Castle – Britwell (Kidderminster Road). (RT)
447	Redhill – Doods Road – Reigate – Earlswood – Redhill – Merstham (Delabole Road) and Reigate – Earlswood – Redhill – South

Merstham – Woldingham (two sections). Withdrawn between South Merstham and Woldingham (covered by 440/A) with most short journeys starting from Reigate running to Delabole Road. Projections to Pendell Camp withdrawn. RF crew operation retained. Positioning journeys on route 447A via Main Road and 447B via Blackborough Road no longer run to Woldingham.

467A	New Sunday afternoon route Sidcup – Dartford (Bow Arrow Lane) (RT)
487	Gravesend (Gypsy Corner) – Swanscombe (Craylands Lane). Extended in Swanscombe to Alkerden Lane.
487A	Rosherville – Swanscombe (Craylands Lane). Extended in Swanscombe to Alkerden Lane.
804	New route Pinnacles (works journeys) – Harlow (Bus Station) – Bush Fair via Second Avenue, Tripton Road and Tawneys Road. Projections from Bush Fair to Potter Street and Epping for crew requirements. (RT)

Reigate's routes 440 and 440A both gained an extension to Woldingham replacing the rural projection of route 447 on 13th May 1959 when they were converted to one-man operation. RF 560 is seen in Redhill heading for Woldingham. *Alan B. Cross/ Allen T. Smith*

In addition routes 438 and 439A were converted to RF OMO and 452 lost its GS type in favour of OMO RFs. In St Albans, journeys on routes 304, 355 and 365 proceeding to City Station and route 382 to Codicote were re-routed away from the main section of St Peters Street to run via Hatfield Road and Upper Lattimore Road. Hospital service 851 now conveyed passengers locally over the section between Horley and Smallfield.

The Grays one-man operation met a problem with route 375 on account of the shortness of the route. It was just seven minutes running time from Rainham Crossing to the Ferry and it did not prove possible to reach an agreement with the trade union on a revised method of working. Under the standard agreement the stand time at each terminal had to be a minimum of five minutes which meant that the operation was extremely uneconomic. An experiment was tried with a pavement conductor to collect the fares before passengers boarded. London Transport also failed to reach an agreement with Murex Works to provide the service on a "guaranteed journey" basis, i.e. the company subsidising the service. The route ran for the last time on 30th June with the works transport going to a private contractor. A knock-on effect of this was that on 14th October 1959 one-man operation at Grays was discontinued with routes 374 and 399 going to RT operation.

Part two of the summer programme was introduced on 10th June 1959 as follows:

301 Watford Junction – Aylesbury. School journeys projected from Watford to Aldenham Road (Bushey Mill Lane) via Bushey & Oxhey Stn.

301C Tring or Durrants Farm Estate – Hemel Hempstead (St Pauls Road) or Maylands Avenue. Journey from Durrants Farm Estate to Apsley Mills provided and most Saturday journeys curtailed at Hemel Hempstead Bus Station (see 316).

314A Bennetts End (loop) – Warners End (Hollybush Lane) or Gadebridge (Howard Drive). Extended in Warners End to Birch Green and former Howard Drive journeys extended via Galley Hill to Birch Green.

314B Warners End (Hollybush Lane) or Gadebridge (Howard Drive) – Hemel Hempstead (Maylands Avenue). Revised as route 314A at Warners End.

316 Chesham – Hemel Hempstead (Highfield, Bathurst Road). Curtailed at Hemel Hempstead (Bus Station) and projected on Saturday to St Pauls Road.

319A Two Waters – Nash Mills – Kings Langley Station – Abbots Langley (works journeys). Reinstated between Abbots Langley and Garston Garage.

319C Ovaltine Works – Apsley Mills – Two Waters Garage (works journeys). Extended from Ovaltine Works to Garston Garage and from Two Waters Garage to Hemel Hempstead (Bus Station).

On 10th June 1959 route 316 lost its projection to Bathurst Road, Hemel Hempstead. GS 17, seen in Chesham heading for Hemel Hempstead Bus Station, appears to be doing little business. *F.W. Ivey*

Routes 350 and 350A from Bishops Stortford to Hertford were converted from RT to RF one-man operation on 10th June 1959 when they acquired a lengthy extension over route 342 to New Barnet. Hertford's allocation of RT2s which were required for route 327 frequently appeared on other routes and in this picture, RT 62 is seen on route 350A heading for Bishops Stortford. Hertford lost its RT2s on 1st September 1957. *Alan B. Cross*

322 Watford Junction – Hemel Hempstead (Bus Station) with projections to The Parade. Extended to Highfield (Bathurst Road) to cover route 316 and converted from RF crew to RF OMO.

322A New Sunday only route Watford Junction – Warners End (Birch Green) via Gadebridge Road and Galley Hill. (RF OMO)

322B New Saturday afternoon route Watford Junction – Kings Langley (The Nap) via route 322 to Ovaltine Works. (RF OMO)

324 Welwyn Garden City circular in both directions Knightsfield – Cherry Tree – Ludwick Way – Hollybush Lane – Howlands – Heronswood Road – Welwyn Garden City Station with certain journeys continuing to Knightsfield. Sunday journeys to Lemsford Lane reinstated.

342 New Barnet – Hertford route withdrawn, covered by extension of routes 350/A.

350 Hertford – Bishop's Stortford (Havers Lane Estate) via Wareside. Extended from Hertford to New Barnet Station. Projections to Horns Mill via County Hall and to Sele Farm Estate from the Ware direction retained. Horns Mill projections via West Street withdrawn. Converted from RT to RF OMO operation.

350A Hertford – Bishop's Stortford (Havers Lane Estate) via Stanstead Abbots. Extended from Hertford to New Barnet Station. Projections to Horns Mill via County Hall from the Ware direction retained. Converted from RT to RF OMO operation.

371A Purfleet Station – Tilbury (Feenan Highway) via West Thurrock and Dock Road. Certain Sunday journeys amended to run to Tilbury Ferry.

377 Boxmoor Station – Friars Wash via St Johns Road route number withdrawn. The one remaining journey to Boxmoor runs as 377A.

378 Warners End (Martindale Road) or Boxmoor (Wharf Road) – Apsley Mills works journeys. Certain journeys extended in Warners End to Birch Green.

381 Epping Garage – Toothill. Extended from Epping to Roydon.

The conversion of route 322 to one-man operation at Two Waters also enabled the Saturday only 307B to be similarly converted. In addition to the above alterations buses on routes 384 and 384B were re-routed at Stevenage to either terminate at or double run via the Bus Station. In Bishop's Stortford route 386 was extended from South Road to Havers Lane Estate. In Harlow the last section of the original routeing of route 393 was withdrawn when buses were re-routed away from Netteswell Cross to run direct via First Avenue. The seasonal extension of Sunday service to Whipsnade Zoo on route 313 commenced on 10th June, or possibly a fortnight earlier, and lasted until 11th October. The Monday to Friday service ran from 22nd July to 15th September inclusive. The Sunday double running to Whipsnade Zoo on route 337 commenced on 14th June and lasted until 11th October on which date route 364A was curtailed at Kensworth for the winter.

On 8th July 1959 some alterations in Slough saw the withdrawal of route 457B (Trading Estate – Slough – Upton Lea circular) to be replaced by new RT worked circular route 400 Britwell (Wentworth Avenue) – Farnham Road – Slough – Upton Lea loop returning via Slough to Britwell. Unlike the 457B, buses worked in both directions around the Upton Lea loop and certain journeys from the Slough direction terminated at Trading Estate. Buses on the 484 group were withdrawn between Britwell and Farnham Road (George). The use of the number 484C for buses terminating at the Trading Estate was discontinued with buses using the numbers 484/A/B according to the origin.

Due to the closure of Napsbury Station certain Wednesday journeys on route 338 were extended from Harperbury Hospital to Radlett Station and a new Sunday and Wednesday hospital route 338A was introduced on 16th September 1959 running from St Albans Garage to Radlett Station via Kings Road (London Colney) and Napsbury Gates.

The winter programme was introduced on 14th October 1959 when the following route alterations applied:

309   Rickmansworth – Harefield (St Mary's Road) or Hill End. Extended from Rickmansworth to Chorleywood (Furze View) via The Swillet with projections to Chorleywood (The Gate) in replacement for route 361. Journeys to Truesdale Drive retained.

325A   St Albans (Firbank Road) – Cottonmill Estate (Abbots Avenue). Journey provided from New Greens Estate (Woollam Crescent) to Cottonmill Estate.

346E   Oxhey Estate (Heysham Drive) – Aldenham Road (Bushey Mill Lane) school service. Extended to Garston (St Michael's School) via Watford By-Pass and St Albans Road.

347   Hemel Hempstead (Bus Station) – Uxbridge. Certain Sunday journeys projected to Two Waters Garage.

361   Rickmansworth – Chorleywood (Green Street) with projections to The Gate route withdrawn.

362A   New Sunday route Ley Hill – High Wycombe via Widmer End introduced in consequence of withdrawal of Sunday service on the 366. (RT)

388   Sawbridgeworth – Hertford – Tewin – Welwyn and projections to Mardley Hill. Certain journeys re-routed at Welwyn North Station to run to Welwyn Garden City Station via Black Fan Road.

Slough local route 457B was revised and renumbered 400 on 8th July 1959. In this view taken shortly before the route's withdrawal RT 4543 attracts a large queue of would-be passengers.
Alan B. Cross

407 Windsor – Slough Trading Estate via Bath Road route withdrawn, covered by revised 446B.

407B Windsor – Slough Trading Estate via Stoke Road, Elliman Avenue and Whitby Road one journey only in this direction – use of route number withdrawn, journey renumbered 446.

446B Slough Station – Trading Estate via Bath Road. Revised to run from Windsor (Bus Station) or Slough Station to the Trading Estate.

487 Gravesend (Gypsy Corner) – Swanscombe (Alkerden Lane). Extended from Gypsy Corner to Singlewell (Hever Court Estate).

489 Ash – Gravesend via Westwood, Southfleet with one journey projected to Singlewell (George). The Singlewell journey was revised to run to Hever Court Estate.

In addition a number of intermediate rerouteings were made. Route 337 was re-routed in Studham away from unclassified direct road via Common Road, Valley Road and Church Road. In Hatfield routes 341A and 389 were re-routed away from Roe Green Lane and Meadow Dell to run direct from St Albans Road to Cavendish Way as route 340B. In Stevenage route 392A was re-routed away from a section of Six Hills Way and Homestead Moat to run via St Georges Way and the full length of Cuttys Lane. Route 393 was re-routed between Great Parndon and Harlow Bus Station to run via Third Avenue instead of Hare Street. In Crawley journeys on route 426A to Ifield (Bonnetts Lane) were withdrawn. The morning special journey on route 424 from Crawley (Bus Station) to Blackwell County Primary School was revised to terminate at Stone Quarry Estate, double running via the school. The North & North East area timetable booklet contained details of a new route 375 from St Albans Garage to How Wood Estate via The King Harry and Park Street. The route, which was never introduced, would have had to be single-deck worked in order to pass under the railway bridge at Park Street. It was to appear as 355A in the following year.

By the time of the introduction of the winter programme for 1959 all Country Bus RFs had been converted for one-man operation. The decision was made that three of the busiest routes (391/A, 447 group and 458) would remain crew operated using Green Line RFs which had been released from relief duties by the substitution of RTs. The allocation book for 14th October 1959 shows the following crew-operated single-deck routes. With the exception of the above routes the duties were probably worked with a crew for scheduling requirements. In some cases the vehicles concerned might have worked on other routes and in certain instances RF coaches might have been used:

Route	Garage	Mon-Fri	Sat	Sun
352	TG	-	1a	-
387	TG	1a	-	-
391/A	SA	7b	7	4
392/A	SV	2	2c	1
406C	RG	1	-	-
419	LH	1d	-	5e
421	DG	1	-	-
434/73	CY	-	1	-
434/73	EG	-	1	1
447/A/B	RG	7f	8f	4
458	WR	7	8	4
466	ST	-	1	-
Dup.	CY	1a	-	-
Works	DG	1	-	-
Dup.	EG	1a	1a	-
Works	WY	1	-	-
Total		31d	30	19

Notes:
a   Worked by 15T13
b   Includes route 325A Mon-Fri
c   Includes one duplicate
d   Plus one additional on Monday
e   Hospital traffic
f   Plus one RLH

A minor fares revision took place on 23rd August 1959 when most 6d fares inside the Special Area were increased to 7d. This was, however, only a precursor to a major increase of fares which applied from 1st November 1959. All fares of between 8d and 2s 1d were increased by 1d with higher fares being increased by up to a maximum of 5d. Halfpenny units were abolished for children's half fares with fractions of 1d being charged as 1d. Previously the child rate for the adult minimum fare of 3d had been 1½d but 2d was now charged. The existing 9d and 11d Early Morning Single fares were withdrawn with a new range of between 1s 0d and 1s 6d applying. There were the usual exceptions for certain routes or sections of routes outside the Special Area and where other operators' fare scales applied.

RT 4200 is seen on Gravesend local route 495 heading for Christianfields Estate. The bus still displays five lines of intermediate points and has been fitted with flashing indicators – a fairly rare combination. *Ken Glazier*

Country bus operation was by no means always through leafy lanes. The north Kent trunk route 480 between Erith and Gravesend serving a lot of Thames-side industry was extremely busy. In this evening peak scene taken in March 1959 RT 2507 runs through Crayford bound for Denton. Trolleybuses have been lined up ready to cope with the mass exodus from nearby Vickers Works.
Alan B. Cross

During 1959 the bus RFs on the crew operated 447 group were all fitted for one-man operation and replaced by Green Line vehicles. RF 566 is seen working the circuitous route 447 prior to the change.
Alan B. Cross/Allen T. Smith

At the end of 1959 Tring Garage still retained a 15T13 type for use on route 387 on Monday to Friday and route 352 on Saturday. T 793 is seen at Berkhamsted Station about to depart for Dunstable.
Bus of Yesteryear

As the decade drew to a close London Transport was in rather a different position from which it had been ten years earlier. All pre-war buses had been replaced and as far as Country Buses was concerned there was now a standardised fleet consisting of RT and RF types with special needs being met by the low-height RLH and small saloon GS. The failure of passenger growth to meet levels predicted when the RTs were ordered meant that London Transport had, by the mid-1950s, an embarrassing surplus of double deckers which had led to the premature withdrawal from service of the Cravens bodied RTs. Under the British Transport Commission, the Country Area had been expanded in the east to include Tilbury. One-man operation had been considerably extended in the Country Area with all but three busy single-deck routes or groups of routes being so worked.

In a period of post-war prosperity increased car ownership coupled with the popularity of television meant that demand for bus travel had dropped with services being reduced accordingly, particularly during evenings and on Sunday. The 1958 strike had reduced passenger numbers considerably and the pattern of constant reductions in passenger usage and service levels had become firmly established and would persist throughout the next decade. Shortage of operating staff was also a problem that was here to stay and it was a fine balance between wage increases and fare increases. On the positive side three new garages had been opened in the Country Area at Garston, Hatfield and Stevenage. Ticket issuing had been revolutionised by the replacement of punch tickets by Gibson machines and the introduction of Ultimate machines on the RF OMO routes.

RT 623 is seen reversing into Dumfries Close whilst performing the terminal working at Oxhey Estate, Hallowes Crescent. A bus on route 346 to Watford and Kingswood waits at the boarding point on the opposite side of the road. Route 346B was a Monday to Friday peak hour feeder route for Carpenders Park Station running between the terminals of routes 346 and 346A in Oxhey Estate.
Ron Wellings

At busy times buses were frequently loaned to Dartford Garage and a special arrangement existed whereby blinds showing the route number and destination were produced. This meant that only the front and rear destination blinds needed to be changed instead of all seven. RT 4728 stands opposite Dartford Garage equipped to work the special service to Crayford Ness on route 486. *Alan B. Cross*

The main route 486 ran between Dartford, Fleet Estate to Belvedere. RT 3208 is seen in Dartford. *Alan B. Cross*

RT 3135 passes Kingston Bus Station heading for Bookham Station on route 418. Central Area buses, including a TD, complement this busy scene. *Alan B. Cross*

After the bus strike the loss of passengers in more traditional areas was to some extent balanced by the expansion of routes in the growing new towns. In this view RT 3502 on route 396A is seen opposite Harlow Bus Station on the short run to Hare Street. In the next decade it would be something of a losing battle for passengers between the bus and the motor car. *Ron Wellings*

In the year 1959 Country Buses operated 43.6 million car miles which was nine per cent fewer than in 1954. Some 250.0 million passenger journeys were made which represented a reduction of 15.7 per cent compared with 1954 and 666.9 million passenger miles travelled represented a 12.4 reduction against 1954. Green Line coaches revived after the strike achieving figures comparable to 1957 levels but Country Buses did not.

Financially London Transport's remit was to make a profit and provide an adequate service, two requirements which were gradually coming into conflict. Under the terms of the Transport Act, 1947, London Transport was required to make a considerable contribution to the British Transport Commission's central charges. This annual figure had been increased from £5.5 million in 1957 to £6 million in 1958. After meeting this burden in 1957, London Transport

was left with a surplus of just £208,000. The disastrous strike of 1958 meant that there was a deficit of £4.2 million, but in 1959 after meeting the BTC contribution, London Transport just about broke even with a surplus of a mere £29,000. The contribution to the BTC had not always been met and at the end of 1959 there was an accumulated deficit of £17.2 million.

The basic network of services remained recognisable throughout the 1950s but a vast number of changes were made to serve the new towns and other new housing. In the event Country Buses was now set to alter little with basic route patterns firmly established and there would be no new vehicles for a further six years. The new towns were not yet complete and services would continue to expand. The 1960s would prove an even more challenging decade for Country Buses than the 1950s.

301	Watford Junction - Aylesbury
301a	Watford Junction - Ovaltine Works (works journeys)
301b	Watford Junction - Berkhamsted via Watford By-Pass (works journeys)
301c	Hemel Hempstead - Dudswell
302	Watford Heath - Hemel Hempstead
303	New Barnet - Hitchin via Bell Bar
303a	New Barnet - Hitchin via Brookmans Park Station
303b	Hitchin - Stevenage (Broomin Green) (works journeys)
304	Tyttenhanger - Whitwell - Hitchin
305	Gerrards Cross - Beaconsfield via The Chalfonts
305a	Gerrards Cross - Chalfont Common
306	New Barnet - Leavesden (Ganders Ash or Works) and works journeys to Brockley Hill
307	Boxmoor - Harpenden (Westfield Road)
307a	Apsley Mills - Harpenden (Westfield Road)
308	Hertford - Newgate Street
308a	Hertford - Little Berkhampstead
309	Rickmansworth - Uxbridge
310	Hertford North Station - Enfield Town
310a	Rye House - Enfield Town
311	Leavesden Works or Watford (Chilcott Road) - Shenley
312	Watford (Gammons Lane) - Little Bushey
313	St. Albans - Enfield Town
314	Fleetville - St. Albans - Hemel Hempstead
316	Chesham - Adeyfield
317	Watford - Sarratt - Hemel Hempstead - Little Gaddesden - Berkhamsted
318	Chipperfield - Abbots Langley - Watford - Sarratt or Bucks Hill
318a	Two Waters - Nash Mills - Kings Langley Station - Abbots Langley - Watford (works journeys)
318b	Two Waters - Kings Langley - Chipperfield (positioning journeys)
318C	Two Waters - Apsley Mills - Ovaltine Works - Kings Langley Station (works journeys)
319	Hemel Hempstead - Nettleden - Little Gaddesden
320	Boxmoor - Hemel Hempstead - Adeyfield - Watford
321	Luton - Maple Cross
322	Watford - Hemel Hempstead via Kings Langley Stn
326	Sands (works journeys) - High Wycombe (Mill End Road) - Micklefield Est. (joint with TV 26)
326a	Sands (works journeys) High Wycombe (Mill End Road) - New Bowerdean (joint with TV 26a)
327	Nazeing Gate - Hertford or Stanstead Abbots
329	Hertford - Nup End
329a	Datchworth - Hitchin
330	St. Albans - Welwyn Garden City (Cole Green Lane)
330a	Welwyn Garden City works journeys Cole Green Lane - Black Fan Road
331	Hertford - Buntingford via West Mill or Baughing
332	Cassiobury Park Estate - Bushey Station
333	Hertford - Bengeo - Chapmore End
333b	Hertford - Ware Park Sanatorium
335	Watford (Leavesden Road Garage) - Windsor
336	Watford (Leavesden Road Garage) - Chesham
337	Watford - Sarratt - Hemel Hempstead - Dunstable
338	Sandridge - St. Albans - Napsbury - Middlesex Colony
339	Epping or Coxtie Green - Warley
340	Welwyn Garden City - New Barnet via New Hatfield and Barnet By-Pass
341	St. Albans - Hertford via Bayford Turning
342	New Barnet - Broxbourne via Hertford Heath
343	St. Albans (Marshalswick) - Welham Green
344	Watford (Met Station) - Brockley Rise (works journeys)
345	Leavesden - Watford - Wiggenhall Road - Oxhey - Northwood - Harefield
346	Kingswood - Watford - Bushey Arches - Oxhey - Northwood - Harefield
348	Chesham Moor - Buckland Common or St. Leonards
350	Hertford - Bishop's Stortford via Wareside

350a	Hertford - Bishop's Stortford via Stanstead Abbots
351	St. Albans - Uxbridge
352	Berkhamsted - Dunstable
353	Berkhamsted - Windsor
354	Fleetville - St. Albans - Marshalswick (circular)
355	Borehamwood (Potters Lane) - St. Albans (Lancaster Road) via Radlett
356	Luton - Markyate - Flamstead
358	St. Albans - Borehamwood via Shenley
359	Amersham - Aylesbury (joint with Eastern National)
360	Luton - Caddington
361	Rickmansworth - Chorleywood via The Swillet
362	Ley Hill - High Wycombe via Anne's Corner
362a	Ley Hill - High Wycombe
362b	Penn - Hazlemere - High Wycombe
363	High Wycombe - Totteridge
364	Luton - Hitchin
365	Hill End - St. Albans - Wheathampstead - Luton
366	High Wycombe - Widmer End
368	St. Albans City Stn - Whipsnade Zoo (Summer only)
369	Sandridge - St. Albans - Dunstable
370	Grays - Romford via Upminster
371	Grays - Rainham via Aveley
371a	Grays - Purfleet
372	Hertford - Welwyn Garden City (Lemsford Lane)
373	Penn - Beaconsfield - Holtspur
374	Grays - Uplands Estate - Aveley (Tunnel Garage) with projections to Rainham
375	Rainham Ferry - Rainham with projections to White Post Corner (works journeys)
376	Luton - Kensworth - (Whipsnade Zoo, Summer only)
376a	Kensworth - Dunstable (Sphinx Works) (works journeys)
377	Boxmoor - Markyate (works journeys)
377a	Apsley Mills - Markyate (works journeys)
377b	Apsley Mills - Cupid Green (works journeys)
378	Boxmoor - Apsley Mills (works journeys)
382	Codicote - St. Albans (works journeys City Station to Sandridge)
383	Hitchin - Weston or Purwell Lane Estate
384	Hertford - Letchworth via Dane End
384a	Hertford - Great Munden
384b	Walkern - Letchworth via Letchworth Gate (works journeys)
385	Croxley Green (Manor Way) - Mill Way Estate via Vicarage Road
386	Hitchin - Bishop's Stortford via Braughing
387	Tring (Beaconsfield Road) - Tring Stn - Aldbury
388	Hertford - Mardley Hill via Tewin
389	Hertford - Sawbridgeworth
390	Hertford - Stevenage via Watton
391	Harpenden - Wheathampstead - St. Albans - Hill End
391a	Townsend - St. Albans - Hill End
393	Harlow - Hoddesdon
394	Hyde Heath - Great Missenden via Chartridge
394a	Chesham Moor - Great Missenden via Chartridge
394b	Chesham (Nashleigh Arms) - Great Missenden via Chartridge and Ballinger
394c	Hyde Heath - Amersham (positioning journeys)
395	Ware (Fanshawe Crescent) - Hertford (projected to Watton on Sundays)
395a	Ware (Musley Hill) - Hertford (projected to Watton on Sundays)
396	Epping - Bishops Stortford
397	Tring - Chesham Moor
398	Amersham - Beaconsfield via Coleshill
398a	Amersham - Winchmore Hill via Coleshill (schools journeys)
399	Hertford - Epping - Coopersale Street

401	Sevenoaks - Upper Belvedere or Lower Belvedere
401b	Swanley - Eynsford (positioning journeys)
402	Bromley North Station - Tonbridge (works journeys Fort Halstead - Sevenoaks)
403	Wallington - Tonbridge
403a	Wallington - Warlingham Park Hospital
403b	Wallington - Farleigh
404	Shoreham Village - Sevenoaks
405	West Croydon - Crawley (projections to Three Bridges)
406	Kingston - Redhill
406c	Earlswood - Redhill - Main Road - Reigate - Kingswood (works journeys)
406e	Epsom Town - Epsom Downs (special service)
406f	Epsom Station - Epsom Downs (special service)
408	Guildford - Warlingham (projections to Chelsham)
409	West Croydon - Forest Row
410	Bromley North Station - Reigate
411	West Croydon - Godstone - Reigate
412	Dorking - Holmbury St. Mary (Sutton) or Leith Hill
413	Brasted or Sundridge Hospital - Ide Hill - Sevenoaks - Chipstead
413a	Four Elms - Ide Hill - -Sevenoaks - Chipstead (also Ide Hill - Sundridge Hospital)
	Both routes 413 and 413A have Sunday morning projections from Chipstead to Chevening
414	West Croydon - Horsham via Dorking
415	Guildford - Ripley
416	Leatherhead - Esher
417	Windsor - Langely Village (works projections to Meadfield Road and Colnbrook) and hospital journeys to Old Windsor Emergency Hospital
418	Little Bookham - Kingston via Ashtead Station and Berrylands
418a	418 positioning journeys running via main road (ie not via Ashtead Station)
419	Langley Vale - Epsom - West Ewell
421	Sevenoaks - Heverham
422	Leatherhead - Boxhill
423	Longfield - Crockenhill via Dartford and Birchwood
423a	Dartford - Joyce Green - Wells Factory (hospital and works journeys)
423b	Watchgate - Dartford - Littlebrook (works journeys)
423d	Watchgate - Dartford - Barn End Lane
424	Reigate - East Grinstead (Stone Quarry Estate)
424	Supplementary services Horley - Horne, Horley - Outwood
425	Dorking North Station - Guildford
426	Crawley Circular via Charlwood and Horley
427	Weybridge - Woking via Byfleet and Pyrford Schools
428	East Grinstead - Dormansland via Lingfield
429	Newdigate - Brockham - Dorking
430	Redhill - South Park - Reigate
431	Sevenoaks - Orpington via Chelsfield
431a	Sevenoaks - Orpington via Green Street Green (positioning journeys)
431b	Knockholt Pound - Fort Halstead via Otford Lane (works journeys)
431c	Knockholt Station - Fort Halstead (works journeys)
431d	Orpington - Fort Halstead via Green Street Green (works journeys)
432	Great Bookham - Guildford via Horsley
433	Ranmore Common - Coldharbour via Dorking
434	Edenbridge - Horsham
435	Leatherhead - Tadworth (hospital journeys Stoke D'Abernon - Leatherhead)
436	Staines - Woking via Woodham
436a	Woking - Ripley
436b	Woking - Guildford via Merrow
437	Weybridge - Woking via Byfleet
438	Guildford - Woking via Burpham
439	Redhill - Wray Common - Reigate - Brockham - Dorking - Newdigate
439a	Merstham - Reigate via Wray Common

440	Redhill - Salfords
440a	Redhill - Redstone Estate
441	Staines - High Wycombe or Hedgerley Village
441b	Beaconsfield - Langley Village (works journeys)
441d	Staines - Virginia Water
442	Slough - Farnham Royal via Stoke Poges (summer extension to Burnham Beeches)
443	Staines - Ascot (early journey and race days)
444	Windsor - Slough - Manor Park or Whitby Road
445	Windsor - Datchet Common
446	Farnham Road - Whitby Road - Slough - Bath Road - Farnham Road
446a	Farnham Road - Manor Park - Slough - Bath Road - Farnham Road
446b	Slough Station - Trading Estate via Bath Road (works journeys)
447	Redhill - Doods Road - Reigate - Earlswood - Redhill - South Merstham and Reigate - Earlswood - Redhill - South Merstham - Woldingham (two sections)
447a	Positioning journeys running via Main Road
447b	Positioning journeys running via Blackborough Road
448	Guildford - Ewhurst
450	Dartford - Gravesend via Betsham
451	Hartley Court - Gravesend via Betsham
452	Dartford - Kingsdown via Greenhithe and Longfield
453	Caterham - Warlingham (projections to Chelsham)
454	Chipstead - Bat & Ball - Sevenoaks - Weald - Tonbridge
454a	Chipstead - Tubs Hill Stn - Sevenoaks - Weald - Tonbridge
455	Uxbridge - High Wycombe
455a	Wooburn Common - West Wycombe
455b	Beaconsfield - Cliveden Hospital (hospital service)
456	Weybridge - Woking via New Haw and Pyrford Schools
456b	Addlestone - West Byfleet - Vickers Works - Weybridge - Addlestone (works circular)
457	Windsor - Uxbridge via Uxbridge Road
457a	Windsor - Uxbridge via Upton Lea
457c	Uxbridge - Pinewood (works journeys)
457d	Windsor - Pinewood via Upton Lea (works journeys)
458	Slough - Uxbridge via Langley
460	Staines - Slough via Datchet
461	Walton - Staines
461a	Walton - Ottershaw (hospital projections to Botleys Park)
462	Staines - Leatherhead (also works journeys via Red Hill Road to Wisley)
462b	Vickers Works - Walton (works journeys)
462c	Vickers Works - Ottershaw (works journey)
463	Walton Woking via Woodham
464	Westerham - Holland via Crockham Hill with projections to Staffhurst Wood and Limpsfield
465	Edenbridge - Holland via Crockham Hill with projections to Staffhurst Wood and Limpsfield
466	Staines - Virginia Water via Stroude
467	Sidcup - Horton Kirby or Wilmington via Dartford
468	Chessington Zoo - Epsom - Leatherhead (projected summer Sundays to Effingham)
469	Staines - Virginia Water or Knowle Hill via Pooley Green and Thorpe
470	Dorking - Warlingham (projections to Chelsham)
471	Orpington circular via Cudham and Knockholt
474	Slough - Burnham Beeches (summer Sunday)
475	Crayford Ness - Belvedere (Crabtree Manor Way) (works journeys)
477	Chelsfield - Orpington - Dartford
478	Swanley - Wrotham
479	Farningham - Dartford via Horton Kirby and Darenth
480	Erith - Gravesend (Denton) and works journeys Crayford Ness - Dartford
480a	Rosherville - Denton (works journeys)
481	Dartford - Temple Hill Estate
484	Farnham Road - Slough - Bath Road - Langley Village (or Meadfield Road works journeys)
484a	Farnham Road - Slough - Bath Road - Datchet
484b	Farnham Road - Slough - Bath Road - Colnbrook
484c	Trading Estate - Slough - Bath Road - Colnbrook (works journeys)

485	Westerham - Edenbridge
486	Dartford (Fleet Estate) - Upper Belvedere or Lower Belvedere via Thames Road
487	Gypsy Corner - Swanscombe (Craylands Lane)
487a	Rosherville - Swanscombe (Craylands Lane) (works journeys)
488	Kings Farm Estate - Swanscombe (Eglington Road)
488a	Rosherville - Kings Farm Estate (works Journeys)
489	Ash - Singlewell via Westwood, Southfleet and Gravesend
489a	Meopham (Hook Green) - Gravesend via Westwood and Southfleet
490	Hartley Court - Singlewell via New Barn, Southfleet and Gravesend
490a	Hartley Court - Northumberland Bottom via New Barn and Gravesend
491	Lower Belvedere - Horton Kirby or Wilmington (works journeys to Crabtree Manor Way)
492	Gravesend - Kingsdown via Southfleet and Westwood
494	East Grinstead - Oxted
495	Northfleet - Kings Farm Estate via Waterdales and Parrock Street
495a	Rosherville - Echo Square - Kings Farm Estate (works journeys)
496	Dartford - Northfleet - Kings Farm Estate via Vale Road and Windmill Street
496a	Rosherville - Waterdales (works journeys)
497	Dover Road Schools - Gravesend
497a	Clifton Marine Parade - Dover Road Schools (works journeys)

Route 445 running from Windsor to Datchet Common had been worked by a variety of vehicles ranging from 20-seaters, large saloon single-deckers to double-deckers. RT 998 is seen in Windsor working on the route. The Windsor Garage engineers were always very adept at making up blinds and boards to requirements and have no doubt fabricated the curious style of lettering on the destination blind.
Alan B. Cross

301	Watford Junction - Aylesbury and school journeys to Watford (Aldenham Road)
301a	Watford Junction - Ovaltine Works via Hempstead Road (works journeys)
301b	Watford Junction - Hemel Hempstead or Durrants Farm Estate via Watford By-Pass (works journeys)
301c	Hemel Hempstead (St. Pauls Road) - Durrants Farm Estate or Tring
301d	Watford Junction - Ovaltine Works via Watford By-Pass (works journeys)
302	Watford Heath - Hemel Hempstead (Longlands)
303	New Barnet - Hitchin via Bell Bar
303a	New Barnet - Hitchin via Brookmans Park Station
304	Colney Street or St. Albans City Station - Whitwell with projection to Hitchin
305	Uxbridge - Gerrards Cross - The Chalfonts - Beaconsfield
305a	Gerards Cross - Chalfont Common - Horn Hill
306	New Barnet - Leavesden (Ganders Ash or Works) and works journeys to Aldenham Works
306a	New Barnet - Leavesden (Ganders Ash) via Little Bushey (school journey)
307	Boxmoor - Harpenden (Masefield Road)
307a	Apsley Mills - Harpenden (Masefield Road)
307b	Hemel Hempstead (Bus Station) - Chaulden
308	Hertford - Cuffley
308a	Hertford - Little Berkhampstead
309	Chorleywood - Harefield (Hill End or St. Marys Road)
310	Hertford (Sele Farm Estate) - Enfield Town
310a	Rye House - Enfield Town
311	Leavesden (Ganders Ash or Works) - Shenley
312	Watford (Cassiobury Drive) - Little Bushey
313	Enfield Town - St. Albans extended summer to Whipsnade Zoo
314a	Hemel Hempstead (Warners End) - Bennetts End
314b	Hemel Hempstead (Warners End) - Maylands Avenue (works journeys)
315	Welwyn Garden City (Black Fan Road) - Kimpton
316	Chesham - Hemel Hempstead (Bus Station or St. Pauls Road)
316a	Hemel Hempstead (Bathurst Road) - Apsley Mills (works journeys)
317	Two Waters - Boxmoor - Hemel Hempstead - Little Gaddesden - Berkhamsted
317a	Two Waters - Hemel Hempstead - Nettleden - Little Gaddesden
318	Hemel Hempstead (Bus Station) - Sarratt - Watford - Abbots Langley
318a	Bucks Hill - Watford - Abbots Langley
318b	Garston - North Watford (Maytree Crescent) (school journeys)
319	Watford - Abbots Langley - Chipperfield - Sarratt
319a	Garston - Abbots Langley - Nash Mills - Two Waters (works journeys)
319b	Two Waters - Chipperfield (positioning journeys)
319c	Garston - Abbots Langley - Apsley Mills - Two Waters (works journeys)
319d	Garston - Abbots Langley - Langlebury School (school journeys)
320	Hemel Hempstead (Adeyfield) - Warners End - Gadebridge
321	Luton - Maple Cross and Harpenden - Uxbridge (two sections)
321a	Luton - Rickmansworth (Berry Lane Estate)
322	Watford - Kings Langley Station - Hemel Hempstead(Bathurst Road)
322a	Watford - Kings Langley Station - Hemel Hempstead (Warners End)
322b	Watford Junction - Kings Langley (The Nap)
323	Purfleet - West Thurrock - Grays - Woodside Estate (works journeys)
323a	Purfleet - West Thurrock - Grays - Nutberry Corner (works jounneys)
323b	Purfleet - West Thurrock - Grays - Stifford Clays
324	Welwyn Garden City (Knightsfield) circular
325	St. Albans (New Greens Estate) - Cotton Mill Estate
325a	St. Albans (Firbank Road) - Cotton Mill Estate
326	Sands (works journeys) - High Wycombe (Mill End Road) - Micklefield Est. or New Bowerdean (joint with TV 26/a)
327	Nazeingwood Common - Hertford
328	Rainham or Aveley (Usk Road) - Grays - Woodside Estate with projection to Orsett
328a	Purfleet - Aveley - Grays - Woodside Estate with projection to Orsett (works journeys)
328b	Purfleet - Aveley - Ockendon Station (works journeys)
329	Hertford - Nup End
329a	Datchworth - Hitchin

330   Hemel Hempstead (Bus Station) - Welwyn Garden City (Howlands or Great Gannet)
330b St. Albans - Hatfield (Technical College)
331   Hertford - Buntingford via West Mill or Baughing
332   Amersham Garage - Quill Hall Estate via Stanley hill
333   Hertford - Bengeo - Chapmore End
333b Hertford - Ware Park Sanatorium
334   Hemel Hempstead (Bus Station) - Bennetts End - Maylands Avenue (works journeys)
334a Two Waters - Hemel Hempstead (High Street Green) (works and school journeys)
335   Watford (Leavesden Road) - Windsor
336   Watford (Leavesden Road) - Chesham and school journeys to Watford (Aldenham Road)
336a Rickmansworth - Loudwater Estate
337   Two Waters or Boxmoor - Hemel Hempstead - Dunstable (summer double run to Whipsnade Zoo)
338   Sandridge - St. Albans - London Colney - Radlett
338a St. Albans - Napsbury - Radlett
339   Epping or Coxtie Green - Warley
340   Welwyn Garden City Station - New Barnet via New Hatfield and Barnet By-Pass
340a Potters Bar - Hatfield (Technical College)
340b Welwyn Garden City Station or Birchwood Estate - New Barnet via South Hatfield and Barnet By-Pass
341   St. Albans (Marshalswick) - Hertford via Bayford Turning
341a St. Albans (Marshalswick) - South Hatfield
343   Dunstable - Brookmans Park Station
343a Studham - Dunstable (AC Delco Works) (works journeys)
345   Bushey Station - Napsbury Hospital (hospital service)
346   Kingswood - Watford - Oxhey Estate (Hallowes Cresent)
346a Kingswood - Watford - Oxhey Estate (Heysham Drive)
346b Oxhey Estate (Hallowes Cresent) - Heysham Drive
346d Oxhey Estate (Hallowes Cresent) - Aldenham Road (Bushey Mill Lane) (school journeys)
346e Oxhey Estate (Heysham Drive) - Garston (St. Michaels School) (school journeys)
347   Hemel Hempstead (Bus Station) - Uxbridge
347a Watford (Town Centre) - North Watford - Bushey Station (school journeys)
348   Chesham Moor - Buckland Common or St. Leonards
348a Chesham - Pond Park Estate
349   Grays - Shell Haven - Coryton (works journeys)
350   New Barnet - Bishop's Stortford (Havers Lane Estate) via Hertford and Wareside
350a New Barnet - Bishop's Stortford (Havers Lane Estate) via Hertford and Stanstead Abbots
352   Berkhamsted - Dunstable
353   Berkhamsted - Windsor and journeys to Dudswell
354   St. Albans (Marshalswick) circular
355   Borehamwood (Cowley Hill) - Radlett - St. Albans - Wheathampstead - Harpenden
357   Tilbury (Iron Bridge) - Nutberry Corner - Grays (works journeys)
358   St. Albans - Borehamwood via Shenley
359   Amersham - Aylesbury (joint with United Counties)
360   Luton - Caddington
362   Ley Hill - High Wycombe via Hazlemere
362a Ley Hill - High Wycombe via Widmer End
363   Penn - Hazlemere - High Wycombe - Totteridge
364   Hitchin - Luton - Flamstead
364a Hitchin - Luton - Kensworth extended summer to Whipsnade Zoo
365   St. Albans (City Station) - Wheathampstead - Luton
366   High Wycombe - Widmer End
367   Tilbury Docks - Bata Shoe Factory (works journeys)
368   Grays - Bata Shoe Factory (works journeys)
369   Aveley (Usk Road) - Ockendon Station
370   Tilbury Ferry - Romford via Upminster
370a Tilbury Ferry - Purfleet (works journeys)
371   Rainham - Aveley - West Thurrock - Grays - Tilbury (Feenan Highway)
371a Purfleet - West Thurrock - Grays - Tilbury (Feenan Highway) (works journeys)
371b Rainham - Sandy Lane - Aveley - West Thurrock - Grays - Tilbury (Feenan Highway)
372   Epping (Coopersale Street) - Hertford - Welwyn Garden City (Lemsford Lane)
373   Penn - Beaconsfield - Holtspur

APPENDIX 3   LIST OF NORTHERN AREA ROUTES AS AT 31st DECEMBER 1959

374	Linford - Grays - Uplands Estate - Aveley (Tunnel Garage) with projections to Rainham
377a	Boxmoor or Apsley Mills - Hemel Hempstead - Friars Wash (works journeys)
377b	Apsley Mills - St. Albans Hill - Friars Wash (works journeys)
378	Warners End or Boxmoor - Apsley Mills (works journeys)
379	Tilbury Docks - Chadwell St. Mary (works journeys)
381	Roydon - Epping - Toothill
382	Codicote - St. Albans
383	Hitchin - Weston or Purwell Lane Estate
384	Hertford - Letchworth via Dane End
384a	Hertford - Great Munden
384b	Hertford - Letchworth via Dane End and Letchworth Gate (works journeys)
385	Croxley Green (Manor Way) or Holywell Estate - Mill Way Estate - Aldenham Works
385a	Croxley Green (Manor Way) or Holywell Estate or Watford Met Stn - Meriden Estate - Garston
385b	Croxley Green (Manor Way) or Holywell Estate or Watford Met Stn - Garston or Aldenham Works
386	Hitchin - Bishop's Stortford (Havers Lane Estate) via Braughing
387	Tring (Beaconsfield Road) - Tring Stn - Aldbury
388	Sawbridgeworth - Hertford - Tewin - Mardley Hill or Welwyn Garden City Station
389	New Hatfield (Manor Road) - South Hatfield (works journeys)
390	Hertford - Stevenage Station via Watton
391	Sandridge or St. Albans (Firbank Road) - Hill End or Tyttenhanger
391a	St. Albans (New Greens Estate) - Hill End or Tyttenhanger
392	Stevenage Station - Popple Way - Stevenage (Bus Station) or Gunnels Wood Road
392a	Hitchin or Stevenage Station - Steveanage (Bus Station) - Bandley Hill
393	Old Harlow (Green Man) - Hertford - Welwyn Garden City (Lemsford Lane)
394	Hyde End - Chesham - Chartridge - Great Missenden
394a	Chesham Moor - Chesham - Chartridge - Great Missenden
395	Ware (Fanshawe Crescent) - Hertford (Bus Station)
395a	Ware (Fanham Common) - Hertford (Bus Station)
396	Epping - Bishops Stortford
396a	Harlow (Hare Street) or Pinnacles - Old Harlow - Bishops Stortford or Epping
397	Tring - Chesham Moor
398	Amersham (Quill Hall Estate) - Coleshill - Beaconsfield - Holtspur
398a	Amersham (Quill Hall Estate) - Coleshill - Winchmore Hill (school journeys)
399	Bulphan - Grays - Uplands Estate - Aveley (Tunnel Garage)
801	Hitchin or Stevenage Station - Steveanage (Bus Station) - Longmeadow with projection to Girls Grammar School
801A	Stevenage Station - Gunnels Wood Road - Longmeadow (works journeys)
802	Bandley Hill - Bridge Road - Gunnels Wood Road - Bandley Hill circular (works journeys)
803	Welwyn Garden City Station - Uxbridge (express service)
804	Pinnacles - Harlow (Bus Station) - Bush Fair with projection to Epping
805	Epping - Potter Street - Harlow (Bus Station) - Little Parndon or Pinnacles
805a	Epping - Potter Street - Templefields - Harlow Station (works journeys)
806	Little Parndon - Harlow (Bus Station) - Templefields - Harlow Station (works journeys)
807	Letchworth - Weston - Stevenage (Bus Station) - Gunnels Wood Road
808	Longmeadow - Hitchin (hospital service)
811	Longmeadow - Hitchin (express service)

400	Britwell - Slough - Wexham Court Farm Estate - Slough - Britwell (circular)
401	Sevenoaks - Upper Belvedere or Lower Belvedere and projections to Belvedere Generating Station and Crabtree Manor Way
401b	Swanley - Eynsford (positioning journeys)
402	Bromley North Station - Tonbridge (works journeys Fort Halstead - Sevenoaks)
403	Wallington - Tonbridge and express section West Croydon - Chelsham
403a	Wallington - Warlingham Park Hospital
403b	Wallington - Farleigh
404	Shoreham Village - Sevenoaks
405	West Croydon - Horsham via Crawley (projection to Three Bridges)
405a	Horsham - Roffey Corner via Littlehaven and projection to Crawley
406	Kingston - Redhill
406a	Kingston Tadworth via Merland Rise and express section Kingston - Tadworth
406c	Reigate - Meadvale - Earlswood - Redhill - Main Road - Reigate - Kingswood (works journeys)
406e	Epsom Town - Epsom Downs (race days)
406f	Epsom Station - Epsom Downs (race days)
408	Guildford - Chelsham
408a	Guildford - Merrow (Bushy Hill)
409	West Croydon - Forest Row
410	Bromley North Station - Reigate
411	West Croydon - Godstone - Reigate
412	Dorking North Station - Holmbury St. Mary (Sutton)
413	Brasted or Sundridge Hospital - Ide Hill - Sevenoaks - Chipstead and Sunday morning projections from Chipstead to Chevening
413a	Four Elms - Ide Hill - -Sevenoaks - Chipstead
414	West Croydon - Horsham via Dorking
415	Guildford - Ripley
416	Tadworth or Boxhill - Headley Court - Leatherhead - Esher
417	Windsor - Langely Village (works projections to Meadfield Road and Colnbrook) and hospital journeys to Old Windsor Hospital
418	Little Bookham - Kingston via Ashtead Station and Berrylands
418a	418 positioning journeys running via main road (ie not via Ashtead Station)
419	Langley Vale - Epsom (Brettgrave)
420	Woking - West Byfleet via Sheerwater
421	Sevenoaks - Heverham
422	Boxhill - Headley - Leatherhead and projection to Esher
423	Longfield - Swanley via Dartford and Birchwood
423a	Watchgate (Ladywood Road) - Dartford - Joyce Green - Wells Factory (hospital and works journeys)
423b	Watchgate (Ladywood Road) - Dartford - Littlebrook (works journeys)
423d	Watchgate (Ladywood Road) - Dartford - Wilmington
424	Reigate - East Grinstead (Stone Quarry Estate)
424	Special journeys Crawley - East Grinstead
425	Dorking North Station - Guildford
426	Crawley Circular via Charlwood and Horley
426a	Ifield Station - Pound Hill (Grattons Drive or Hillcrest Close) and journeys to Hazlewick School
427	Weybridge - Woking via Byfleet and Pyrford Schools
428	East Grinstead - Dormansland via Lingfield
429	Newdigate - Brockham - Dorking
430	Redhill - South Park - Reigate
431	Sevenoaks - Orpington via Chelsfield
431a	Sevenoaks - Orpington via Green Street Green (positioning journeys)
431b	Knockholt Pound - Fort Halstead via Otford Lane (works journeys)
431c	Knockholt Station - Fort Halstead via Polhill Arms (works journeys)
431d	Orpington - Fort Halstead via Green Street Green (works journeys)
432	Great Bookham - Guildford via Horsley

433	Ranmore - Coldharbour via Dorking
434	Edenbridge - Crawley (George) via Crawley Down
436	Staines - Guildford via Woodham and Woking
436a	Staines - Ripley via Woodham and Woking
437	Weybridge - Woking via Byfleet
438	East Grinstead - Crawley via Snow Hill and Tinsley Green (works journeys)
438a	East Grinstead - Crawley via Crawley Down and Tinsley Green (works journeys)
438b	Three Bridges Station - Crawley (Bus Station) - Gatwick Road (Rutherford Way) (works journeys)
438c	East Grinstead - Crawley via Crawley Down, Ridleys Corner and Tinsley Green (works journeys)
439	Redhill - Wray Common - Reigate - Brockham - Dorking - Newdigate
439a	Merstham - Reigate via Wray Common
440	Woldingham - Redhill - Salfords
440a	Woldingham - Redhill - Redstone Estate
441	Staines - High Wycombe or Hedgerley Village
441a	Windsor - Britwell
441b	Beaconsfield - Langley Village (works journeys)
441c	Staines - Englefield Green (Larchwood Drive)
441d	Staines - Virginia Water
443	Staines - Ascot (early journey and race days)
445	Windsor - Datchet Common
446	Slough - Whitby Road - Farnham Road (supplementary journeys via Bath Road)
446a	Slough - Manor Park - Farnham Road (supplementary journeys via Bath Road)
446b	Windsor - Trading Estate via Bath Road (works journeys)
447	Redhill - Doods Road - Reigate - Earlswood - Redhill - South Merstham - Merstham (Delabole Road)
447a	Positioning journeys running via Main Road
447b	Positioning journeys running via Blackborough Road
448	Guildford - Ewhurst
448a	Guildford - Pewley Way
449	Chart Downs Estate - Dorking - Goodwyns Farm Estate or Holmwood
450	Dartford - Gravesend via Betsham
451	Hartley Court - Gravesend via Betsham
452	Dartford - West Kingsdown via Greenhithe and Longfield
453	Caterham - Warlingham (projections to Chelsham)
454	Chipstead - Bat & Ball - Sevenoaks - Weald - Tonbridge
454a	Chipstead - Sevenoaks Stn - Sevenoaks - Weald - Tonbridge
455	Uxbridge - High Wycombe
455a	Wooburn Common - West Wycombe
456	Weybridge - Woking via New Haw and Pyrford Schools
456b	Addlestone - West Byfleet - Vickers Works - Weybridge - Addlestone (works circular)
457	Windsor - Uxbridge via Uxbridge Road also summer express service
457a	Windsor - Uxbridge via Upton Lea
457c	Uxbridge - Pinewood (works journeys)
457d	Windsor - Pinewood via Upton Lea (works journeys)
458	Slough - Uxbridge via Langley
460	Staines - Slough via Datchet
461	Walton - Staines
461a	Walton - Botleys Park
462	Staines - Leatherhead
462a	Stoke D'Abernon - Leatherhead via Leatherhead Court (hospital journeys)
462b	Vickers Works - Walton (works journeys)
462c	Vickers Works - Ottershaw (works journey)
463	Walton - Guildford via Woodham, Woking and Merrow
464	Westerham - Holland via Crockham Hill with projections to Oxted (Barrow Green Road), Staffhurst Wood and Limpsfield.
465	Edenbridge - Holland via Crockham Hill with projections to Staffhurst Wood and Limpsfield
466	Staines - Virginia Water via Stroude
467	Sidcup - Horton Kirby or Wilmington via Dartford

467a   Sidcup - Dartford (Bow Arrow Lane)
468   Chessington Zoo - Epsom - Leatherhead (projection to Effingham)
469   Staines - Virginia Water via Pooley Green and Thorpe
470   Dorking (Bus Station) - Warlingham Park Hospital or Farleigh
471   Orpington circular via Cudham and Knockholt
472   Leatherhead - Netherne Hospital (hospital service)
473   Dormansland - Crawley (George) via Rowfant
475   Crayford Ness - Belvedere (Crabtree Manor Way) (works journeys)
476   Tilgate - Langley Green with projection to Ifield (Parade)
476a   Pound Hill (Hillcrest Close) - Manor Royal - Langley Green - Ifield (Parade)
        (works journeys)
476b   Tilgate - Gatwick Road (Rutherford Way) - Gatwick Airport (works journeys)
477   Chelsfield - Orpington - Dartford (Henderson Drive)
477a   Chelsfield - Orpington - Dartford (Joyce Green Hospital)
478   Swanley (St. Mary's Estate) - Wrotham
480   Erith - Gravesend (Denton)
480a   Rosherville - Denton (works journeys)
481   Epsom Station - Wells Estate
482   Caterham Station - Smallfield Hospital (hospital service)
484   Farnham Road or Trading Estate - Slough - Bath Road - Langley Village (or Meadfield Road
        works journeys)
484a   Farnham Road or Trading Estate - Slough - Bath Road - Datchet
484b   Farnham Road or Trading Estate - Slough - Bath Road - Colnbrook
485   Westerham - Edenbridge
486   Dartford (Fleet Estate) - Upper Belvedere or Lower Belvedere via Thames Road
        also works journeys between Dartford Garage and Crayford Ness
487   Singlewell (Hever Court Estate) - Swanscombe (Craylands Lane)
487a   Rosherville - Swanscombe (Craylands Lane) (works journeys)
488   Kings Farm Estate - Swanscombe (Eglington Road)
488a   Rosherville - Kings Farm Estate (works Journeys)
489   Ash - Gravesend via Westwood and Southfleet and projection to Hever Court Estate
489a   Meopham (Hook Green) - Gravesend via Westwood and Southfleet
490   Hartley Court - Gravesend via New Barn and Southfleet
491   Horton Kirby or Wilmington - Lower Belvedere and projections to
        Belvedere Generating Station and Crabtree Manor Way
493   Englefield Green (Larchwood Drive) - St. Peter's Hospital (hospital service)
494   East Grinstead - Oxted
495   Northfleet - Christianfields Estate via Waterdales and Parrock Street
495a   Rosherville - Echo Square - Christianfields Estate (works journeys)
496   Northfleet - Kings Farm Estate via Vale Road and Windmill Street
496a   Rosherville - Waterdales (works journeys)
497   Gravesend - Dover Road Schools
498   Gravesend - Coldharbour Estate or Northfleet via Painters Ash Estate
499   Dartford - Bow Arrow Lane
851   Three Bridges Station - Smallfield Hospital (hospital service)
852   Crawley (Bus Station) - Horsham via Faygate
853   Poundhill (Hillcrest Close) - Three Bridges - Crawley (Bus Station) - Manor Royal -
        Three Bridges - Poundhill (Hillcrest Close) (circular works service)
853a   Poundhill (Hillcrest Close) - Three Bridges - Crawley (Bus Station) - Manor Royal -
        Gatwick Airport (works journeys)
853b   Poundhill (Hillcrest Close) - Three Bridges - Manor Royal - Gatwick Airport
        (works journeys)
854   Chelsfield Station – Sevenoaks Road – Orpington Station – Ramsden Estate (Petton Grove)
854a   Chelsfield Station – Green Street Green (positioining journeys)

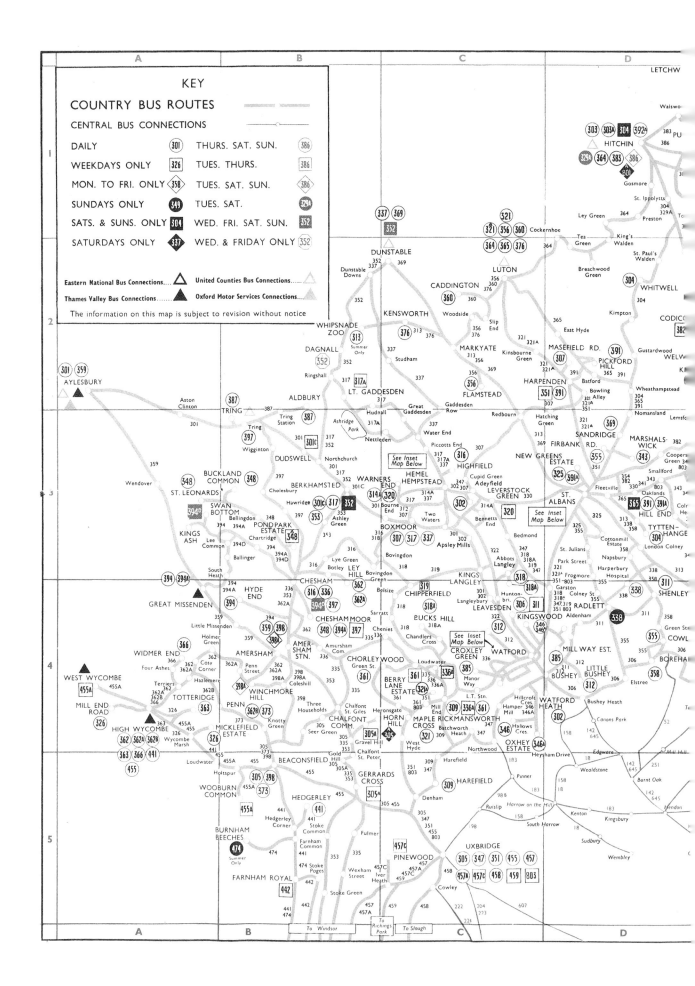

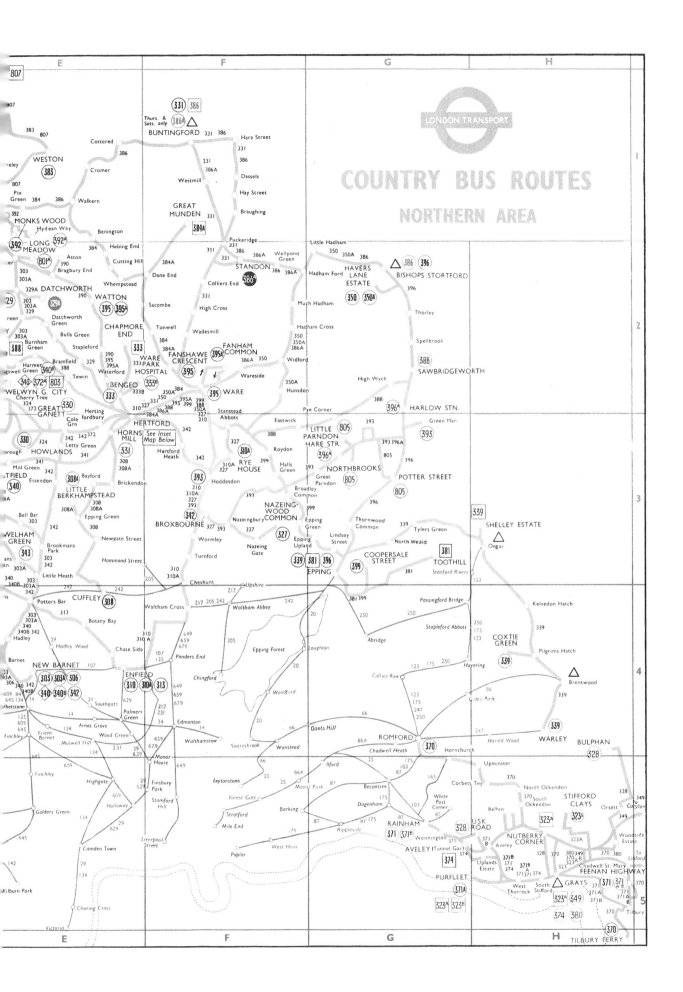

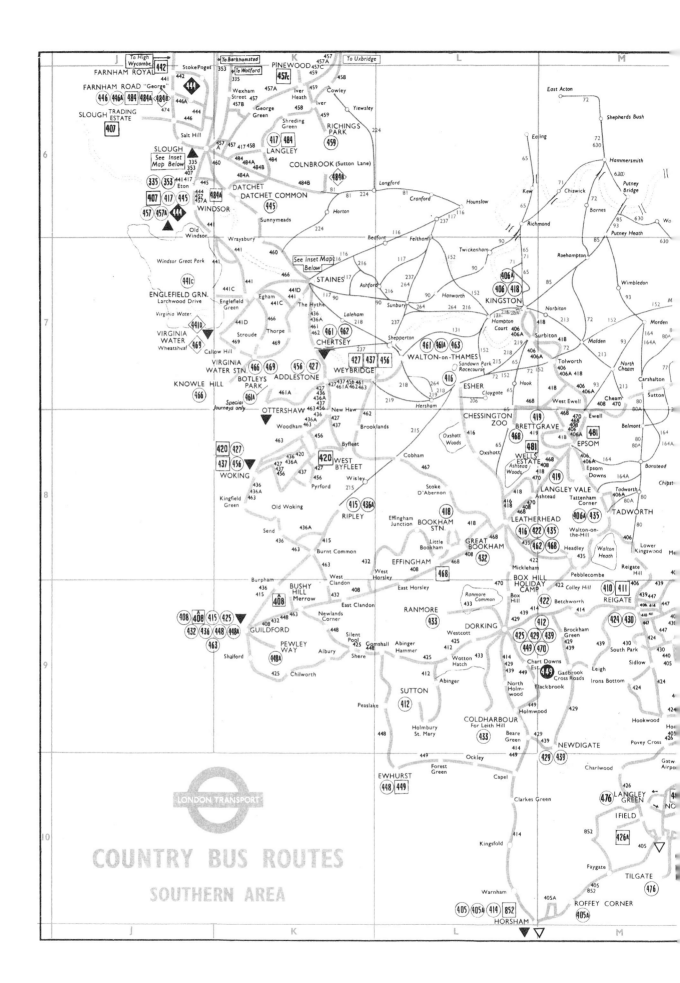

COUNTRY BUS ROUTES

SOUTHERN AREA

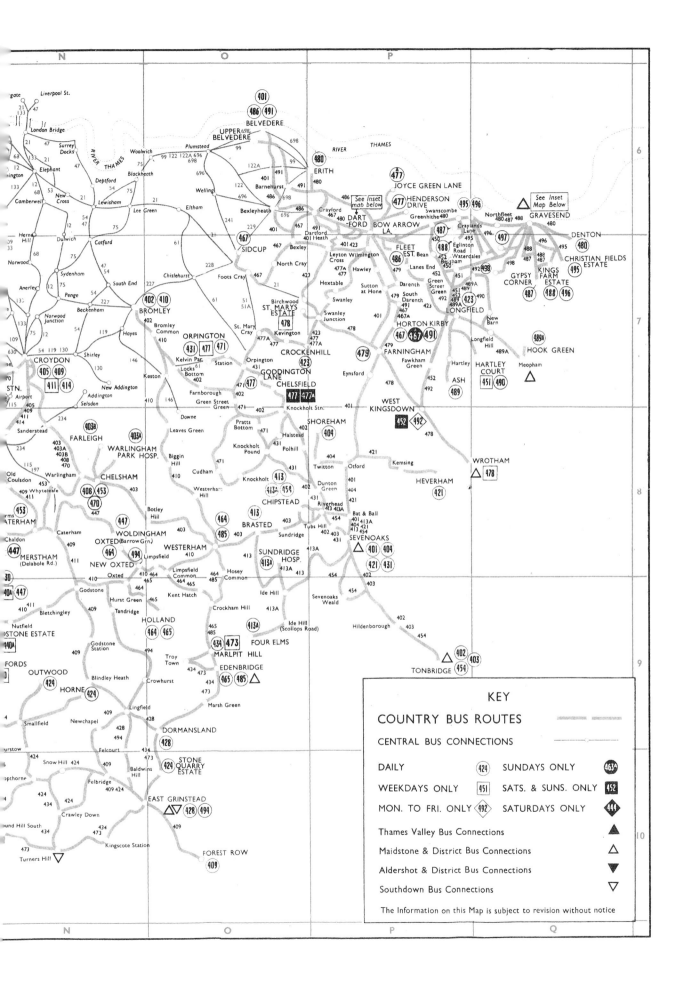

KEY

COUNTRY BUS ROUTES

CENTRAL BUS CONNECTIONS

DAILY	(424)	SUNDAYS ONLY	(463A)
WEEKDAYS ONLY	451	SATS. & SUNS. ONLY	452
MON. TO FRI. ONLY	‹492›	SATURDAYS ONLY	◆444◆

Thames Valley Bus Connections ▲

Maidstone & District Bus Connections △

Aldershot & District Bus Connections ▼

Southdown Bus Connections ▽

The Information on this Map is subject to revision without notice

This scene at Windsor End, Beaconsfield, in August 1954 perhaps epitomises the Country Area in the mid-1950s. RT 3199 bound for Staines on route 441 calls at a 'Keswick' type wooden shelter set against a background of quaint buildings. Motorway construction has today rendered Windsor End a no through road! *London Transport Museum*

The maps on pages 156–159 date from August 1957.